Preface	4
1. Introduction to Progressive Web Apps	6
1.1 What are Progressive Web Apps?	7
1.2 Benefits of Progressive Web Apps	11
1.3 Core Technologies of Progressive Web Apps	15
1.4 Overview of Vue.js for Progressive Web Apps	19
2. Overview of Vue.js	24
2.1 Introduction to Vue.js	25
2.2 Core Features of Vue.js	29
2.3 Vue.js Architecture	35
2.4 Setting Up a Vue.js Project	41
3. Setting Up Your Development Environment	45
3.1. Installing Node.js and npm	46
3.2. Setting Up Vue CLI	49
3.3. Configuring Your Editor and Plugins	53
3.4. Project Structure and Files	57
4. Creating Your First Vue.js App	63
4.1 Setting Up Your Development Environment	64
4.2 Installing Vue CLI	67
4.3 Creating a New Vue.js Project	70
4.4 Running and Exploring Your App	74
5. Implementing Progressive Web App Features	78
5.1 Introduction to Service Workers	79
5.2 Adding Offline Support	83
5.3 Implementing Push Notifications	88
5.4 Enhancing Performance and Security	93

6. Working with Vue.js Components — 99

- 6.1 Introduction to Vue.js Components — 100
- 6.2 Creating Your First Component — 104
- 6.3 Component Communication — 110
- 6.4 Advanced Component Patterns — 116

7. Managing State with Vuex — 122

- 7.1 Introduction to Vuex — 123
- 7.2 Core Concepts of Vuex — 128
- 7.3 Managing State with Vuex Stores — 135
- 7.4 Advanced Vuex Techniques — 142

8. Integrating Service Workers — 149

- 8.1 Understanding Service Workers — 150
- 8.2 Registering a Service Worker — 154
- 8.3 Caching Strategies — 158
- 8.4 Updating and Debugging Service Workers — 163

9. Handling Offline Capabilities — 168

- 9.1 Overview of Offline Capabilities — 169
- 9.2 Service Workers and Caching Strategies — 174
- 9.3 Handling Data Synchronization — 178
- 9.4 Managing Offline Notifications — 183

10. Performance Optimization Techniques — 190

- 10.1 Code Splitting and Lazy Loading — 191
- 10.2 Efficient State Management — 196
- 10.3 Optimizing Network Performance — 201
- 10.4 Utilizing Browser Caching — 208

11. Testing and Debugging Your PWA — 214

- 11.1 Setting Up Your Testing Environment — 215

11.2 Unit Testing Vue Components	*219*
11.3 End-to-End Testing with Cypress	*225*
11.4 Debugging Common Issues	*229*

12. Glossary — 235

Glossary for "Building Progressive Web Apps with Vue.js" — **236**

Preface

Welcome to "Building Progressive Web Apps with Vue.js." In an era where seamless user experiences and high performance are imperative, Progressive Web Apps (PWAs) stand out as a hybrid solution combining the best of web and mobile apps. This book aims to take you on a journey through the world of PWAs, providing you with the essential knowledge and tools needed to build robust and efficient web apps using Vue.js.

You may be wondering, why this book? The need for reliable, fast, and engaging web applications has never been more critical. PWAs address this need by offering capabilities like offline access, push notifications, and background sync, making web apps more app-like. Vue.js, on the other hand, is a progressive JavaScript framework that focuses on the view layer, making it approachable yet powerful enough to handle complex single-page applications.

This book is unique in its AI-generated content, bringing you a structured, informative, and comprehensive guide to mastering PWAs with Vue.js. Each chapter is designed to build upon the previous one, ensuring a smooth learning curve as we progress from basic concepts to advanced techniques.

Here's a quick preview of what you'll learn:

1. **Introduction to Progressive Web Apps**
   Understand the fundamentals of PWAs and why they are revolutionary.

2. **Overview of Vue.js**
   Get introduced to Vue.js and its core features.

3. **Setting Up Your Development Environment**
   Learn how to set up a development environment tailored for building PWAs with Vue.js.

4. **Creating Your First Vue.js App**
   Step-by-step guidance to build your first Vue.js application.

5. **Implementing Progressive Web App Features**
   Discover how to integrate essential PWA features into your Vue.js app.

6. **Working with Vue.js Components**
   Dive deep into Vue.js components and how to effectively use them.

7. **Managing State with Vuex**
   Learn how to manage application state using Vuex.

8. **Integrating Service Workers**
   Understand the role of Service Workers in PWAs and how to implement them.

9. **Handling Offline Capabilities**
   Ensure your app stays functional even when offline.

10. **Performance Optimization Techniques**
    Optimize your PWA for maximum performance.

11. **Testing and Debugging Your PWA**
    Methods for testing and debugging to ensure your app is bug-free and reliable.

12. **Glossary**
    A handy glossary to quickly look up important terms and concepts.

We hope this book serves as a valuable resource in your journey to create exceptional Progressive Web Apps using Vue.js. Embrace the power of modern web development and elevate your skills with this comprehensive guide.

Happy coding!

1. Introduction to Progressive Web Apps

1.1 What are Progressive Web Apps?

Progressive Web Apps (PWAs) represent a unique approach to web application development that aims to combine the best features of both web and native apps. PWAs offer enhanced user experiences similar to native mobile apps while maintaining the accessibility and ease of deployment associated with web applications.

Characteristics of Progressive Web Apps

Progressive

The term "progressive" highlights the idea that these apps work for every user, regardless of their browser choice, because they are built with progressive enhancement as a core tenet.

Responsive

PWAs are designed to fit any form factor, whether it be a desktop, mobile, tablet, or even devices yet to emerge. This adaptability ensures a seamless user experience across a range of devices.

Connectivity-Independent

One of the most powerful features of PWAs is their ability to function offline or under poor network conditions. This capability is achieved through service workers, which cache essential resources and manage network requests.

App-like

By leveraging an app shell model, PWAs offer an app-like experience. They employ minimal navigational elements and a focus on high performance for smoother user interactions.

Fresh

PWAs are always up-to-date, thanks to service workers that automatically update the app when resources are available in the background.

Safe

Operating through HTTPS ensures the security of PWAs by preventing snooping and ensuring the content hasn't been tampered with.

Discoverable

PWAs are identifiable as "applications" thanks to W3C manifests and service worker registration, enabling search engines to index them.

Re-engageable

With features like push notifications, PWAs can interactively engage users, helping to bring them back to the application.

Installable

PWAs can be easily installed to the home screen of a user's device without the need to visit an app store, offering a native app-like experience and increasing user retention.

Example: Basic App Shell

The app shell model is fundamental to creating PWAs. Here's a basic example of an HTML skeleton to illustrate the core structure of an app shell:

```html
<!DOCTYPE html>
<html lang="en">
<head>
    <meta charset="UTF-8">
    <meta name="viewport" content="width=device-width, initial-scale=1.0">
    <link rel="manifest" href="manifest.json">
    <link rel="stylesheet" href="styles.css">
    <title>My PWA</title>
</head>
<body>
    <header>
        <nav>
            <h1>My Progressive Web App</h1>
        </nav>
    </header>
    <main>
        <section id="content">
            <!-- Dynamic content goes here -->
        </section>
    </main>
    <script src="main.js"></script>
</body>
</html>
```

Service Worker Registration

Service workers are a cornerstone of PWAs, enabling offline capabilities and background syncing. Below is a simple example of how to register a service worker in your application:

```
<script>
    if ('serviceWorker' in navigator) {
        window.addEventListener('load', () => {
            navigator.serviceWorker.register('/service-worker.js')
                .then((registration) => {
                    console.log('ServiceWorker registration successful with scope: ', registration.scope);
                }, (error) => {
                    console.log('ServiceWorker registration failed: ', error);
                });
        });
    }
</script>
```

Summary

Progressive Web Apps offer a multitude of benefits by combining the best of web and native app functionalities. They are designed to be fast, reliable, and engaging under various network conditions and on different devices. By leveraging technologies like service workers and app shells, PWAs aim to deliver superior user experiences, enabling developers to reach a broader audience with minimal effort.

In subsequent sections, we will delve deeper into the benefits, core technologies, and how Vue.js can be used to create robust Progressive Web Apps.

1.2 Benefits of Progressive Web Apps

Progressive Web Apps (PWAs) have revolutionized the way users experience web applications by bridging the gap between web and native mobile apps. This unique approach combines the best of both worlds, providing a seamless, reliable, and engaging user experience. Let's delve into the myriad benefits PWAs offer, especially when built using Vue.js.

Cross-Platform Compatibility

One of the standout features of PWAs is their ability to run on any platform with a modern web browser. This means you write your code once and it works everywhere, from desktops to smartphones to tablets. With Vue.js, a versatile and approachable JavaScript framework, building cross-platform PWAs becomes even more efficient.

```
// vue.config.js
module.exports = {
  pwa: {
    name: 'My PWA',
    themeColor: '#4DBA87',
    msTileColor: '#000000',
    manifestOptions: {
      background_color: '#FFFFFF'
    }
  }
};
```

Offline Functionality

PWAs can be used even without an internet connection. This offline capability is enabled through Service Workers, which cache essential resources and data. Vue.js can be integrated seamlessly with Service Workers to enhance offline support.

```js
// registerServiceWorker.js
if (process.env.NODE_ENV === 'production') {
  window.addEventListener('load', () => {
    navigator.serviceWorker
      .register('/service-worker.js')
      .then((registration) => {
        console.log('ServiceWorker registration successful with scope: ', registration.scope);
      })
      .catch((error) => {
        console.log('ServiceWorker registration failed:', error);
      });
  });
}
```

Improved Performance

PWAs are designed to load quickly and perform efficiently. By taking advantage of caching strategies and lazy loading, PWAs ensure minimal loading time and smooth operation. Vue.js supports a variety of tools and techniques to optimize performance, such as code-splitting and pre-fetching.

```
// example component lazy loading
const Home = () => import(/* webpackChunkName: "home" */ '.
/views/Home.vue');

export default new Router({
  routes: [
    {
      path: '/',
      name: 'Home',
      component: Home,
    },
  ],
});
```

App-like Feel

PWAs offer an app-like experience with features such as home screen installation, push notifications, and full-screen mode. When used with Vue.js, you can leverage its component-based architecture to create a modular and scalable application that feels like a native app.

```
<!-- Example of meta tags for fullscreen mode in index.html
-->
<meta name="mobile-web-app-capable" content="yes">
<meta name="apple-mobile-web-app-capable" content="yes">
```

Discoverability

Unlike native apps, PWAs are easily discoverable through search engines. They utilize SEO-friendly URLs and can be shared via links, ensuring a broader audience reach. Vue.js's router allows easy creation of dynamic and optimized URLs.

```js
// router.js
const routes = [
  { path: '/', component: Home },
  { path: '/about', component: About },
  { path: '/contact', component: Contact },
];

const router = new VueRouter({
  mode: 'history',
  routes,
});

export default router;
```

Cost-Effective Development

Developing a single PWA that works on all devices can be more cost-effective than developing multiple platform-specific apps. This efficiency is enhanced with Vue.js due to its flexibility, ease of learning, and extensive community support.

```json
// package.json
{
  "name": "my-pwa",
  "version": "1.0.0",
  "dependencies": {
    "vue": "^2.6.11",
    "vue-router": "^3.1.3",
    // other dependencies
  },
  // other configurations
}
```

Automatic Updates

PWAs ensure that users always have the latest version of the app without needing to manually update it. Service Workers automatically fetch and install updates in the background.

```js
// service-worker.js (example of using Workbox for automatic updates)
import { precacheAndRoute } from 'workbox-precaching';

precacheAndRoute(self.__WB_MANIFEST);

self.addEventListener('message', (event) => {
  if (event.data && event.data.type === 'SKIP_WAITING') {
    self.skipWaiting();
  }
});
```

PWAs represent a significant advancement in web technology by providing a host of benefits that improve user experience, performance, and development efficiency. By combining these strengths with the power of Vue.js, developers can create robust, high-performance applications that are accessible to a wide audience. This chapter will further explore how to leverage Vue.js to build state-of-the-art Progressive Web Apps.

1.3 Core Technologies of Progressive Web Apps

Progressive Web Apps (PWAs) leverage several core technologies that make them stand out from traditional web applications. These technologies enable PWAs to deliver a user experience that rivals native mobile apps, with benefits such as improved performance, offline capabilities, and enhanced user engagement. The foundational technologies of PWAs include Service Workers, Web App Manifests, and HTTPS.

Service Workers

Service Workers are at the heart of what makes a PWA "progressive." They are a type of web worker, which means they run in the background, separate from the main browser thread, enabling features such as background synchronization, push notifications, and offline caching.

Registering a Service Worker

To begin using a Service Worker, you need to register it in your web application. This is typically done in your main JavaScript file:

```
if ('serviceWorker' in navigator) {
  window.addEventListener('load', () => {
    navigator.serviceWorker
      .register('/service-worker.js')
      .then((registration) => {
        console.log('Service Worker registered with scope:', registration.scope);
      })
      .catch((error) => {
        console.log('Service Worker registration failed:', error);
      });
  });
}
```

Basic Service Worker Lifecycle

A basic lifecycle of a Service Worker includes installation, activation, and fetching. Below is an example of a Service Worker script (`service-worker.js`):

```js
const CACHE_NAME = 'my-pwa-cache-v1';
const urlsToCache = [
  '/',
  '/styles/main.css',
  '/script/main.js'
];

self.addEventListener('install', event => {
  event.waitUntil(
    caches.open(CACHE_NAME)
      .then(cache => {
        return cache.addAll(urlsToCache);
      })
  );
});

self.addEventListener('activate', event => {
  event.waitUntil(
    caches.keys().then(cacheNames => {
      return Promise.all(
        cacheNames.filter(cacheName => {
          return cacheName !== CACHE_NAME;
        }).map(cacheName => {
          return caches.delete(cacheName);
        })
      );
    })
  );
});

self.addEventListener('fetch', event => {
  event.respondWith(
    caches.match(event.request)
      .then(response => {
        return response || fetch(event.request);
      })
  );
});
```

Web App Manifests

A Web App Manifest is a JSON file that provides the browser with information about your web application, such as its name, icons, start URL, and display configuration. The manifest file enables your app to be installed on a device's home screen, providing a more native-like experience.

Example of a Web App Manifest

Here is an example of a simple `manifest.json` file:

```
{
  "name": "My Progressive Web App",
  "short_name": "MyPWA",
  "start_url": "/index.html",
  "display": "standalone",
  "background_color": "#ffffff",
  "theme_color": "#000000",
  "icons": [
    {
      "src": "images/icon-192x192.png",
      "type": "image/png",
      "sizes": "192x192"
    },
    {
      "src": "images/icon-512x512.png",
      "type": "image/png",
      "sizes": "512x512"
    }
  ]
}
```

To link this manifest file in your HTML, add the following `<link>` element in the `<head>` section:

```
<link rel="manifest" href="/manifest.json">
```

HTTPS

Progressive Web Apps require a secure context to operate reliably, mainly because Service Workers and other advanced APIs like Geolocation are only available over HTTPS. HTTPS ensures that data is encrypted during transit, providing a secure communication channel between the user and the server.

Enforcing HTTPS

To ensure your PWA is always served over HTTPS, you can set up a redirect from HTTP to HTTPS on your server. Here's a basic example using Express.js in Node.js:

```
const express = require('express');
const app = express();

// Redirect HTTP to HTTPS
app.use((req, res, next) => {
  if (req.header('x-forwarded-proto') !== 'https') {
    res.redirect(`https://${req.header('host')}${req.url}`);
  } else {
    next();
  }
});

app.use(express.static('public'));

app.listen(3000, () => {
  console.log('Listening on port 3000');
});
```

By leveraging these core technologies—Service Workers, Web App Manifests, and HTTPS—you can create a more reliable, engaging, and secure progressive web application. This foundation enables your app to provide a seamless user experience, offline functionality, and enhanced performance, akin to native mobile applications.

1.4 Overview of Vue.js for Progressive Web Apps

Progressive Web Apps (PWAs) represent a modern web development approach that aims to deliver a native app-like experience for users. These apps utilize web technologies but offer enhancements such as offline support, push notifications, and improved performance. Vue.js, a popular JavaScript framework, can be an excellent tool for building such applications. This subchapter delves into how Vue.js integrates with the concept of Progressive Web Apps and discusses its advantages and features.

Why Choose Vue.js for PWAs?

Vue.js is a flexible and easy-to-learn JavaScript framework that simplifies the development of web applications. Combining Vue.js with PWA principles results in applications that are not only high-performing but also maintainable and scalable. Here are some reasons to choose Vue.js for your PWA development:

- **Ease of Learning**: Vue.js has a gentle learning curve, making it accessible for developers at all levels.
- **Component-Based Architecture**: Vue.js promotes the use of reusable components, enhancing maintainability.
- **Reactive Data Binding**: Its reactivity system allows for efficient data management and UI updates.
- **Strong Ecosystem**: Vue.js's ecosystem includes tools and libraries like Vue CLI for project scaffolding, Vue Router for routing, and Vuex for state management.
- **Integration with Modern Tooling**: Vue.js seamlessly integrates with modern JavaScript tooling and libraries, such as service workers and Webpack, which are essential for building PWAs.

Core Concepts of Vue.js

To effectively use Vue.js for building PWAs, it's important to understand its core concepts:

Components

Vue.js is built around a component-based architecture, where each UI element is a self-contained component. This modularity simplifies the construction and maintenance of complex applications.

Example of a Vue component:

```vue
<template>
  <div class="hello-world">
    <h1>{{ title }}</h1>
    <p>{{ message }}</p>
  </div>
</template>

<script>
export default {
  name: 'HelloWorld',
  data() {
    return {
      title: 'Hello, World!',
      message: 'Welcome to your first Vue component.'
    };
  }
};
</script>

<style scoped>
.hello-world {
  text-align: center;
}
</style>
```

Reactive Data Binding

Vue.js's reactivity system ensures that the DOM stays in sync with the application's state, making it easy to manage dynamic data.

Example of reactive data binding:

```
<template>
  <div>
    <input v-model="message" placeholder="Type something" />
    <p>The message is: {{ message }}</p>
  </div>
</template>

<script>
export default {
  data() {
    return {
      message: ''
    };
  }
};
</script>
```

Vue CLI

Vue CLI is an indispensable tool when building PWAs with Vue.js. It provides a robust setup to scaffold projects and comes with PWA support out of the box.

To create a new Vue.js project with PWA support:

```
npm install -g @vue/cli
vue create my-pwa
cd my-pwa
vue add pwa
```

Service Workers in Vue.js

Service workers are vital for PWAs, enabling features like offline access and push notifications. Vue CLI simplifies service worker integration with its PWA plugin.

Example of a basic service worker registration:

```
if ('serviceWorker' in navigator) {
  window.addEventListener('load', () => {
    navigator.serviceWorker.register('/service-worker.js').
then(registration => {
      console.log('ServiceWorker registration successful wi
th scope: ', registration.scope);
    }).catch(error => {
      console.log('ServiceWorker registration failed: ', er
ror);
    });
  });
}
```

When you run the Vue CLI PWA project, it includes a pre-configured service worker file (`service-worker.js`). You can customize it according to your needs.

Caching Strategies

Vue.js, in conjunction with service workers, allows implementing various caching strategies to enhance the performance and availability of your PWA.

Example of a basic caching strategy:

```javascript
self.addEventListener('install', event => {
  event.waitUntil(
    caches.open('my-app-cache').then(cache => {
      return cache.addAll([
        '/',
        '/index.html',
        '/style.css',
        '/app.js'
      ]);
    })
  );
});

self.addEventListener('fetch', event => {
  event.respondWith(
    caches.match(event.request).then(response => {
      return response || fetch(event.request);
    })
  );
});
```

Conclusion

Vue.js brings together the simplicity and power required to build robust, performant PWAs. By leveraging its component-based architecture, reactive data binding, and strong ecosystem, developers can efficiently create applications that deliver an exceptional user experience. As we move forward, the following chapters will explore more about setting up the development environment, creating a Vue.js application, and implementing various PWA features.

2. Overview of Vue.js

2.1 Introduction to Vue.js

Vue.js is a progressive JavaScript framework primarily used for building user interfaces and single-page applications. It was created by Evan You, and its first release was in February 2014. Vue.js is designed to be incrementally adaptable, meaning you can use it as a simple library to enhance parts of a web page or as a full-fledged framework to build complex applications.

Why Choose Vue.js?

Vue.js offers several reasons why developers might choose it over other frameworks:

- **Simplicity and Ease of Use:** Vue.js comes with a gentle learning curve. Its syntax is clean and intuitive, making it accessible even to beginners.
- **Versatility:** Whether you need to enhance an existing application or build something from scratch, Vue can handle both scenarios efficiently.
- **Performance:** Vue optimizes reactivity using a fine-grained dependency tracking system. This ensures updates to the DOM are efficient.
- **Size:** Vue's core library is lightweight, making your applications faster to load.
- **Ecosystem:** Vue has a robust ecosystem, including tools like Vue Router for routing and Vuex for state management.

Key Features of Vue.js

Some of the key features of Vue.js include:

- **Reactive Data Binding:** Vue uses a reactivity system to automatically update the DOM when data changes. This simplifies the task of keeping the view in sync with the data.
- **Component System:** Vue's component-based architecture allows you to build encapsulated, reusable pieces of UI.
- **Directives:** Vue provides a range of built-in directives (like `v-if`, `v-for`, and `v-bind`) to perform common tasks in templates.
- **Single-File Components:** In Vue, you can define a component's HTML, JavaScript, and CSS all within a single `.vue` file.
- **Transitions and Animations:** Vue includes features for applying animations and transitions when elements enter or leave the DOM.

Getting Started with Vue.js

Let's go through a simple example to see how Vue.js works. Suppose we want to create a simple counter app:

Create an HTML file named `index.html`:

```html
<!DOCTYPE html>
<html lang="en">
<head>
  <meta charset="UTF-8">
  <meta name="viewport" content="width=device-width, initial-scale=1.0">
  <title>Vue.js Counter App</title>
</head>
<body>
  <div id="app">
    <p>{{ message }}</p>
    <button @click="count++">You clicked me {{ count }} times.</button>
  </div>

  <!-- Include Vue.js -->
  <script src="https://cdn.jsdelivr.net/npm/vue@2/dist/vue.js"></script>
  <script>
    new Vue({
      el: '#app',
      data: {
        message: 'Hello Vue!',
        count: 0
      }
    });
  </script>
</body>
</html>
```

Breaking Down the Example

In the example above, we have the following key parts:

13. **HTML Template:**
    - The `<div id="app">` serves as the root element for our Vue instance.
    - The `{{ message }}` syntax is used for data binding to display the message.
    - The button uses Vue's event directive `@click` to listen for click events and update the `count` data property.

14. **Including Vue.js:**
    - The script tag includes Vue.js from a CDN. You can also install it via npm for more complex setups.
15. **Vue Instance:**
    - A new Vue instance is created and mounts to the element with the id app.
    - The `data` object contains the reactive properties `message` and `count`.

Vue.js ensures the view is automatically updated when data properties change. This reactive binding eliminates the need for manual DOM manipulation.

Conclusion

Vue.js's simplicity, flexibility, and performance make it an ideal choice for modern web development. Its learning curve is gentler compared to some other frameworks, and its powerful features provide everything you need to build dynamic and responsive web applications.

In the following sections, we will dive deeper into the core features of Vue.js, explore its architecture, and learn how to set up a Vue.js project.

2.2 Core Features of Vue.js

Vue.js is a progressive JavaScript framework for building user interfaces. It is designed from the ground up to be incrementally adaptable. The core library is focused on the view layer only, making it easy to integrate with other libraries or existing projects. In this section, we will delve into the fundamental features that make Vue.js popular among developers.

Declarative Rendering

Vue.js uses a concise, declarative syntax for rendering data to the DOM. With the help of its template syntax, Vue lets you bind the rendered DOM to the underlying data model.

```
<div id="app">
  {{ message }}
</div>

<script>
new Vue({
  el: '#app',
  data: {
    message: 'Hello Vue.js!'
  }
});
</script>
```

Reactive Data Binding

One of the standout features of Vue.js is its reactivity system. Vue automatically keeps the DOM in sync with the data. When the data changes, the DOM updates accordingly without any manual intervention.

```html
<div id="app">
  <input v-model="message" placeholder="Edit me">
  <p>The input value is: {{ message }}</p>
</div>

<script>
new Vue({
  el: '#app',
  data: {
    message: 'Hello Vue.js!'
  }
});
</script>
```

Component-Based Architecture

Vue.js encourages a component-based architecture where the UI is built using encapsulated, reusable components. This helps in maintaining the codebase and encourages modularity.

```html
<div id="app">
  <greeting></greeting>
</div>

<script>
Vue.component('greeting', {
  template: '<h1>Hello from a component!</h1>'
});

new Vue({
  el: '#app'
});
</script>
```

Single File Components (SFCs)

Vue.js provides a mechanism to define components in a single file using the .vue extension. This file format encapsulates the HTML, JavaScript, and CSS of the component, making it easier to manage.

```vue
<template>
  <div class="greeting">
    <h1>{{ message }}</h1>
  </div>
</template>

<script>
export default {
  data() {
    return {
      message: 'Hello from a Single File Component!'
    };
  }
};
</script>

<style scoped>
.greeting {
  font-family: Arial, sans-serif;
}
</style>
```

To include a single file component, you can import it into your main Vue instance or another component.

```js
import Greeting from './Greeting.vue';

new Vue({
  el: '#app',
  components: {
    Greeting
  }
});
```

Directives

Vue.js provides a set of built-in directives that offer extended functionality in the template syntax. Commonly used directives include v-if, v-for, v-bind, and v-on.

```html
<div id="app">
  <p v-if="isVisible">Now you see me!</p>
  <ul>
    <li v-for="item in items" :key="item.id">{{ item.text }}</li>
  </ul>
  <button v-on:click="toggleVisibility">Toggle Visibility</button>
</div>

<script>
new Vue({
  el: '#app',
  data: {
    isVisible: true,
    items: [
      { id: 1, text: 'Item 1' },
      { id: 2, text: 'Item 2' },
      { id: 3, text: 'Item 3' }
    ]
  },
  methods: {
    toggleVisibility() {
      this.isVisible = !this.isVisible;
    }
  }
});
</script>
```

Vue CLI

Vue.js offers a command-line interface (CLI) for rapid project scaffolding. It provides instant project setup along with best practices, enabling developers to focus on writing code rather than configuring their development environment.

```
npm install -g @vue/cli
vue create my-project
```

For more details, you can visit the official documentation at https://cli.vuejs.org.

Vue Router

Vue Router is the official library for integrating client-side routing in Vue.js applications. It allows you to map routes to components and manages the navigation and history of the application.

```
import Vue from 'vue';
import VueRouter from 'vue-router';
import Home from './components/Home.vue';
import About from './components/About.vue';

Vue.use(VueRouter);

const routes = [
  { path: '/', component: Home },
  { path: '/about', component: About }
];

const router = new VueRouter({
  routes
});

new Vue({
  el: '#app',
  router,
  render: h => h(App)
});
```

Vuex

Vuex is the state management pattern and library for Vue.js applications. It serves as a centralized store for all the components in an application, making state management more predictable and easier to debug.

```javascript
import Vue from 'vue';
import Vuex from 'vuex';

Vue.use(Vuex);

const store = new Vuex.Store({
  state: {
    count: 0
  },
  mutations: {
    increment(state) {
      state.count++;
    }
  }
});

new Vue({
  el: '#app',
  store,
  computed: {
    count() {
      return this.$store.state.count;
    }
  },
  methods: {
    increment() {
      this.$store.commit('increment');
    }
  }
});
```

These core features form the backbone of Vue.js, making it a versatile and powerful framework for building progressive web applications. In the next sections, we will dive deeper into Vue.js architecture and the steps to set up a Vue.js project.

2.3 Vue.js Architecture

Vue.js is a progressive JavaScript framework primarily used for building user interfaces. One of the key reasons for its widespread adoption is its flexible and efficient architecture. This subchapter delves into the architecture of Vue.js, explaining its core components, the principles it adopts, and how everything fits together to create a robust and engaging user experience.

Reactive Data Binding

At the heart of Vue.js architecture is its reactivity system. This system ensures that the UI stays in sync with the data.

Reactivity System

Vue.js leverages a reactivity system based on a plain JavaScript object. When you define a Vue instance, the data object is converted into reactive properties. This means that any change to these properties will trigger a UI update.

```
new Vue({
  data: {
    message: "Hello Vue!"
  }
});
```

In the example above, `message` is a reactive property. If it changes, Vue.js will automatically update the DOM to reflect the new value.

Component-Based Structure

Vue.js encourages a component-based architecture, which helps in breaking down the UI into smaller, reusable pieces.

Single-File Components

Vue.js uses Single-File Components (SFCs) to encapsulate HTML, JavaScript, and CSS in one file with the `.vue` extension. This encapsulation facilitates better organization and maintainability.

```
<template>
  <div class="greeting">
    <h1>{{ message }}</h1>
  </div>
</template>

<script>
export default {
  data() {
    return {
      message: "Hello Vue!"
    };
  }
}
</script>

<style scoped>
.greeting {
  color: blue;
}
</style>
```

Vue Instance Lifecycle

The Vue instance goes through a series of initialization steps when it is created. These steps allow developers to insert custom behavior at different stages of an instance's lifecycle.

Lifecycle Hooks

Vue.js provides various lifecycle hooks that let you add custom behavior at crucial points in an instance's lifecycle.

```js
new Vue({
  data: {
    message: "Hello Vue!"
  },
  created() {
    console.log('Vue instance has been created');
  },
  mounted() {
    console.log('Vue instance has been mounted');
  },
  updated() {
    console.log('Vue instance has been updated');
  },
  destroyed() {
    console.log('Vue instance has been destroyed');
  }
});
```

Vue Router

For handling navigation, Vue.js offers an official routing library called Vue Router. It allows you to define routes and map them to your components.

```js
const routes = [
  { path: '/home', component: HomeComponent },
  { path: '/about', component: AboutComponent }
];

const router = new VueRouter({
  routes
});

new Vue({
  router,
  render: h => h(App)
}).$mount('#app');
```

In the above example, `VueRouter` is configured with routes pointing to `HomeComponent` and `AboutComponent`. These routes can be navigated within the application without a full page reload.

Vuex for State Management

Vuex is a state management pattern designed specifically for Vue.js applications. It centralizes component state, making it easier to manage data.

Store Structure

In Vuex, the store is the global state management point. It contains the state, mutations for synchronous state modifications, actions for asynchronous tasks, and getters for retrieving state data.

```js
const store = new Vuex.Store({
  state: {
    count: 0
  },
  mutations: {
    increment(state) {
      state.count++;
    }
  },
  actions: {
    increment(context) {
      context.commit('increment');
    }
  },
  getters: {
    count: state => state.count
  }
});

new Vue({
  store,
  computed: {
    count() {
      return this.$store.getters.count;
    }
  },
  methods: {
    increment() {
      this.$store.dispatch('increment');
    }
  }
}).$mount('#app');
```

Vue CLI

Vue CLI is a tool for quickly scaffolding Vue.js projects with preset or custom configurations. It simplifies the setup of modern front-end tooling and is highly extensible.

```
npm install -g @vue/cli
vue create my-vue-app
```

The above commands will install Vue CLI globally and create a new Vue.js project with the name my-vue-app. Vue CLI offers various features like plugins, an instant prototype, and a graphical user interface for managing projects.

Plugins and Directives

Vue.js also supports plugins and directives, which extend its functionality.

Custom Directives

Directives are special tokens in the markup that tell the library to do something to a DOM element.

```
Vue.directive('focus', {
  inserted: function (el) {
    el.focus();
  }
});

new Vue({
  template: '<input v-focus>'
}).$mount('#app');
```

In this example, a custom directive v-focus is defined, which automatically focuses on the input element when it is inserted into the DOM.

Conclusion

Vue.js's architecture is designed to give developers a powerful yet flexible framework for building interactive UIs. With its reactivity system, component-based structure, lifecycle hooks, Vue Router, Vuex, Vue CLI, and support for plugins and directives, Vue.js provides all the tools needed for creating progressive web apps. Understanding how these components interact will enable you to harness the full potential of Vue.js in your applications.

2.4 Setting Up a Vue.js Project

Setting up a Vue.js project is the first step toward building a Progressive Web App (PWA) using this versatile framework. In this subchapter, we'll walk through the necessary steps to get a Vue.js project up and running using Vue CLI, along with instructions for configuring and running your new project.

Installing Vue CLI

The Vue Command Line Interface (CLI) is an essential tool when starting a Vue.js project. It provides an efficient way to scaffold new projects and comes with a range of features and plugins for rapid development.

To begin, you'll need Node.js and npm (Node Package Manager) installed on your machine. You can download and install them from the official Node.js website: https://nodejs.org/

After installing Node.js and npm, you can install Vue CLI globally by running the following command in your terminal:

```
npm install -g @vue/cli
```

Creating a New Vue.js Project

Once Vue CLI is installed, you can create a new Vue.js project using the `vue create` command. Open your terminal and run:

```
vue create my-vue-pwa
```

You'll be prompted to choose a preset. For a PWA, it's recommended to select the "Vue 3 + Babel + ESLint" preset. Follow the prompts to set up your project structure. Alternatively, you can manually select features by choosing the "Manually select features" option. Make sure to include the PWA support if you're planning to add progressive features to your app.

Understanding the Project Structure

After the project is created, navigate to the project directory:

```
cd my-vue-pwa
```

The project structure will look something like this:

```
my-vue-pwa/
├── node_modules/
├── public/
├── src/
│   ├── assets/
│   ├── components/
│   ├── App.vue
│   └── main.js
├── .gitignore
├── babel.config.js
├── package.json
├── README.md
└── vue.config.js
```

- **public/**: Static assets that are not processed by Webpack.
- **src/**: Your main application code.
    - **assets/**: Static assets that are processed by Webpack.
    - **components/**: Vue.js components.
    - **App.vue**: The root component.
    - **main.js**: The entry point where Vue is initialized.
- **.gitignore**: Specifies which files to ignore in the repository.
- **babel.config.js**: Babel configuration.

- **package.json**: Project metadata and dependencies.
- **README.md**: Project documentation.
- **vue.config.js**: Vue CLI configuration (optional).

Running the Development Server

To see your new Vue.js project in action, start the development server by running:

```
npm run serve
```

Open your web browser and navigate to http://localhost:8080/. You should see a welcome message from Vue.js, indicating that your project is up and running.

Customizing the Configuration

Vue CLI allows you to customize the project configuration via the `vue.config.js` file. Common customizations include modifying the dev server settings, tweaking Webpack configurations, and enabling specific plugins.

Here's a simple example of a `vue.config.js` file that customizes the dev server port:

```
module.exports = {
  devServer: {
    port: 3000
  }
};
```

Adding PWA Support

To add PWA support to your Vue.js project, you need to install the PWA plugin:

```
vue add pwa
```

This will modify the project structure and configuration files to include the necessary PWA attributes such as `manifest.json` and service workers.

Conclusion

By now, you've successfully set up a Vue.js project and are ready to start developing your Progressive Web App. In the upcoming chapters, we will delve deeper into building components, managing state, and integrating PWA features to create a high-performance, offline-capable web application.

3. Setting Up Your Development Environment

3.1. Installing Node.js and npm

Node.js and npm (Node Package Manager) are essential tools for modern JavaScript development, including building Progressive Web Apps (PWAs) with Vue.js. Node.js provides a runtime environment for executing JavaScript outside of a browser, while npm allows you to manage and install libraries, frameworks, and other dependencies. This subchapter will guide you through the installation process for both.

Downloading Node.js and npm

16. **Visit the Node.js website**: Open your browser and navigate to the official Node.js website: https://nodejs.org.

17. **Choose the appropriate version**: You'll see two versions available for download: the LTS (Long-Term Support) version and the Current version.

    - The **LTS version** is recommended for most users, especially for those starting new projects or using Node.js in production environments.
    - The **Current version** includes the latest features but may be less stable.

18. **Download the installer**: Click the appropriate link to download the installer for your operating system (Windows, macOS, or Linux).

Installing Node.js and npm on Windows

19. **Run the installer**: Once the download is complete, double-click the installer to launch it.

20. **Follow the installation wizard**: The installation wizard will guide you through the setup process. Accept the default settings unless you have specific requirements.

21. **Verify the installation**: After the installation is complete, open your Command Prompt and run the following commands to verify that Node.js and npm were installed correctly: `node -v`

    `npm -v`

    You should see version numbers displayed for both Node.js and npm, indicating that the installation was successful.

Installing Node.js and npm on macOS

22. **Run the installer**: Double-click the downloaded `.pkg` file to open the installer.

23. **Follow the installation wizard**: The wizard will guide you through the setup. Again, accept the default settings unless you need to customize the installation.

24. **Verify the installation**: Open Terminal and run: `node -v`

    `npm -v`

    These commands should display the installed versions of Node.js and npm.

Installing Node.js and npm on Linux

25. **Using a package manager**: Depending on your Linux distribution, install Node.js and npm using your package manager. For Debian-based distributions like Ubuntu, run: `sudo apt update     sudo apt install nodejs npm`

26. **Verify the installation**: Check the installed versions by running: node -v

    npm -v

Updating npm

It's often useful to update npm to the latest version even if you have installed the latest Node.js version:

```
npm install -g npm
```

Troubleshooting Common Issues

- **Non-existent npm command**: If you encounter errors indicating that the npm command is not found, ensure that the installation directory is included in your system's PATH environment variable.
- **Permission issues on Linux/macOS**: You might encounter permission issues when installing global modules. If so, you can use the following command with sudo: sudo npm install -g <package-name>

By completing these steps, you ensure that your development environment for building Progressive Web Apps with Vue.js is correctly set up with Node.js and npm. Next, we'll set up the Vue CLI, which will further streamline your workflow.

3.2. Setting Up Vue CLI

To effectively build and manage Vue.js applications, especially Progressive Web Apps, we will use the Vue Command Line Interface (CLI). Vue CLI is a powerful tool that simplifies the process of scaffolding new projects, managing dependencies, and adding essential features. This section provides step-by-step instructions on installing and utilizing Vue CLI for your project.

Installation

Before installing Vue CLI, ensure that you have Node.js and npm set up on your development environment. If you haven't installed these yet, refer to the previous section, "3.1. Installing Node.js and npm."

To install Vue CLI, you will use npm. Run the following command in your terminal:

```
npm install -g @vue/cli
```

This command installs Vue CLI globally on your system, allowing it to be accessed from any directory.

Verifying Installation

After installation, you can verify that Vue CLI is properly installed by checking its version:

```
vue --version
```

This should output the version number of the Vue CLI installed, confirming a successful setup.

Creating a New Project

With Vue CLI installed, you can now create a new Vue.js project. Run the following command:

```
vue create my-pwa-app
```

Replace `my-pwa-app` with your preferred project name. Vue CLI then prompts you to choose a preset for the new project. You have two options:

- **Default preset**: A basic configuration with essential features.
- **Manually select features**: Allows you to choose specific features like TypeScript, Router, Vuex, and Progressive Web App (PWA) support.

For this guide, select "Manually select features" to ensure PWA support is included. Use the arrow keys to navigate and the spacebar to select features, then press Enter.

Ensure you select the following features:

- Babel
- Router
- Vuex
- Linter / Formatter
- Progressive Web App (PWA) Support

You can configure other settings based on your project needs.

Navigating the Project Directory

Once Vue CLI completes scaffolding your project, navigate into the newly created directory:

```
cd my-pwa-app
```

Project Configuration Files

Vue CLI generates several files and folders to bootstrap your application. Below are some key files:

- `package.json`: Manages project dependencies and scripts.
- `vue.config.js`: Configures Vue CLI settings.
- `src/`: Contains your application's source code.
- `public/`: Houses static assets and the `index.html` file.

Running Your Application

To launch your application locally and see it in action, run:

```
npm run serve
```

Vue CLI starts a development server and provides a local URL, typically `http://localhost:8080`, where you can view your application in the browser.

Adding PWA Support

If PWA support was not enabled during initial setup, you can still add it. First, navigate to your project directory and install the PWA plugin:

```
vue add pwa
```

You will be prompted to make configurations such as the name of your PWA, theme color, and whether to include a basic or advanced service worker setup. Configure these settings based on your requirements.

Conclusion

Setting up Vue CLI correctly is crucial for an organized and efficient development process. By following the steps outlined, you have now installed Vue CLI, created a new project, and added necessary configurations to start building your Vue.js-based Progressive Web App.

In the next section, we will delve into configuring your editor and plugins to streamline your development workflow.

3.3. Configuring Your Editor and Plugins

A well-configured editor is crucial for an efficient and smooth development workflow, especially when building Progressive Web Apps (PWAs) with Vue.js. In this section, we will discuss how to set up popular editors such as Visual Studio Code (VS Code) and WebStorm, and the essential plugins that will streamline your development process.

Choosing Your Editor

Selecting the right editor can significantly impact your productivity. Two of the most popular editors among Vue.js developers are VS Code and WebStorm. We'll cover how to set up each of these editors and the essential plugins you should install.

Visual Studio Code (VS Code)

Installation:

27. Download VS Code from https://code.visualstudio.com/
28. Follow the installation instructions based on your operating system.

Essential Extensions:

29. **Vetur**: Vetur is the most popular Vue.js extension for VS Code. It provides Vue syntax highlighting, IntelliSense, debugging support, and more.

    ```
    ext install octref.vetur
    ```

30. **ESLint**: Keep your code clean and consistent by using ESLint. If you followed the instructions in the previous sections, your Vue CLI project will already have ESLint configured.

```
ext install dbaeumer.vscode-eslint
```

31. **Prettier**: This extension automatically formats your code based on a set of defined rules.

    ```
    ext install esbenp.prettier-vscode
    ```

32. **Vue Peek**: This extension allows you to jump to Vue component definitions, making code navigation easier.

    ```
    ext install dariofuzinato.vue-peek
    ```

Configuring the Extensions:

Create a `.vscode/settings.json` file in your project to customize VS Code settings for the project:

```
{
  "vetur.validation.template": false,
  "eslint.validate": ["javascript", "javascriptreact", "vue"],
  "editor.formatOnSave": true,
  "prettier.singleQuote": true,
  "prettier.semi": false
}
```

WebStorm

Installation:

33. Download WebStorm from https://www.jetbrains.com/webstorm/
34. Follow the installation instructions based on your operating system.

Essential Plugins:

35. **Vue.js**: WebStorm provides built-in support for Vue.js. Ensure it's enabled by going to `Preferences > Plugins` and searching for the Vue.js plugin.

36. **ESLint**: Configure ESLint by going to `Preferences > Languages & Frameworks > JavaScript > Code Quality Tools > ESLint`. Set it to automatic configuration.

37. **Prettier**: Install the Prettier plugin from the marketplace and enable it by going to `Preferences > Languages & Frameworks > JavaScript > Prettier`.

Configuring the Plugins:

In WebStorm, open the Preferences and adjust shared settings:

```
{
  "prettier.printWidth": 80,
  "prettier.singleQuote": true,
  "eslint.autoFixOnSave": true,
  "vue.options.api": "composition",
  "typescript.reportStyleErrorsAsWarnings": true
}
```

Customizing Editor Settings

To enhance your development experience, it's essential to tailor your editor settings to suit your needs. Whether you are using VS Code or WebStorm, the setups above will get you started on the right foot.

Recommended Plugins for Enhanced Productivity

Beyond the core plugins, consider the following additional plugins to further boost your productivity:

38. **Path Intellisense**: Autocompletes filenames in your project.

    ```
    ext install christian-kohler.path-intellisense
    ```

39. **Bracket Pair Colorizer 2**: Matches and colors corresponding brackets, making nested code easier to read.

```
ext install CoenraadS.bracket-pair-colorizer-2
```

40. **Auto Close Tag**: Automatically closes HTML and Vue element tags.

    ```
    ext install formulahendry.auto-close-tag
    ```

41. **Auto Rename Tag**: Automatically renames tags for HTML and Vue.

    ```
    ext install formulahendry.auto-rename-tag
    ```

By configuring your editor with these extensions and settings, you'll establish a powerful and efficient development environment that's well-suited for building Progressive Web Apps with Vue.js. Now that your editor is configured, you're ready to dive into creating your first Vue.js app.

3.4. Project Structure and Files

Organizing your project structure properly is crucial for the maintainability and scalability of your Progressive Web App (PWA). When setting up your Vue.js project using Vue CLI, it generates a default project structure that can be customized based on your needs. In this section, we'll go over the significant files and folders created by Vue CLI to help you understand their purposes and how to effectively work with them.

Vue CLI Project Structure

When you create a new Vue project with Vue CLI, you'll typically see a structure similar to this:

```
my-vue-pwa/
├── node_modules/
├── public/
│   ├── favicon.ico
│   └── index.html
├── src/
│   ├── assets/
│   │   └── logo.png
│   ├── components/
│   │   └── HelloWorld.vue
│   ├── views/
│   │   └── Home.vue
│   ├── App.vue
│   └── main.js
├── .gitignore
├── babel.config.js
├── package.json
├── README.md
└── vue.config.js
```

node_modules/

This directory contains all the dependencies and modules installed via npm. You typically do not need to interact with or modify any files within this folder manually.

public/

The public directory contains static assets that are served directly without any processing by Webpack. A key file here is:

- index.html: The main HTML file of your application. You can modify its contents, but Vue will handle injecting the built assets into it.

Example:

```
<!DOCTYPE html>
<html lang="en">
<head>
  <meta charset="UTF-8">
  <meta name="viewport" content="width=device-width,initial-scale=1.0">
  <title>My Vue PWA</title>
</head>
<body>
  <noscript>
    <strong>We're sorry but My Vue PWA doesn't work properly without JavaScript enabled. Please enable it to continue.</strong>
  </noscript>
  <div id="app"></div>
</body>
</html>
```

src/

The src directory is where all your Vue.js application code resides. Understanding the structure and purpose of its contents is vital for effective development.

- **assets/**: Contains static assets like images and stylesheets. Use this folder for assets that need to be processed by Webpack.

Example:

```
/* src/assets/styles.css */
body {
  font-family: 'Arial', sans-serif;
}
```

- **components/**: Contains Vue components, which are reusable parts of the user interface like buttons, forms, or entire sections of a webpage.

Example:

```
<template>
  <div class="hello">
    <h1>{{ msg }}</h1>
  </div>
</template>

<script>
export default {
  name: 'HelloWorld',
  props: {
    msg: String
  }
}
</script>
```

- **views/**: Contains Vue components representing entire views or pages of your application. Use this folder to organize components that are directly mapped to routes.

Example:

```
<template>
  <div class="home">
    <img src="@/assets/logo.png">
    <HelloWorld msg="Welcome to Your Vue.js App"/>
  </div>
</template>

<script>
import HelloWorld from '@/components/HelloWorld.vue';

export default {
  name: 'Home',
  components: {
    HelloWorld
  }
}
</script>
```

- App.vue: The root component of your application. Every Vue app starts from this component.

Example:

```
<template>
  <div id="app">
    <router-view></router-view>
  </div>
</template>

<script>
export default {
  name: 'App'
}
</script>
```

- main.js: The entry point of your application. It initializes Vue and mounts the app to the DOM.

Example:

```
import Vue from 'vue';
import App from './App.vue';
import router from './router';

Vue.config.productionTip = false;

new Vue({
  router,
  render: h => h(App)
}).$mount('#app');
```

Configuration Files

- `.gitignore`: Specifies which files and directories Git should ignore.

Example:

```
node_modules/
dist/
.env
```

- `babel.config.js`: Configuration file for Babel, which is used to transpile modern JavaScript to a version compatible with older browsers.

Example:

```
module.exports = {
  presets: [
    '@vue/cli-plugin-babel/preset'
  ]
};
```

- `package.json`: Lists project dependencies, scripts, and meta-information like the project name and version.

Example:

```json
{
  "name": "my-vue-pwa",
  "version": "0.1.0",
  "scripts": {
    "serve": "vue-cli-service serve",
    "build": "vue-cli-service build",
    "lint": "vue-cli-service lint"
  },
  "dependencies": {
    "vue": "^2.6.11",
    "vue-router": "^3.2.0"
  },
  "devDependencies": {
    "@vue/cli-service": "^4.5.0",
    "@vue/cli-plugin-babel": "^4.5.0"
  }
}
```

- `vue.config.js`: Optional configuration file for Vue CLI, allowing more control over the project's Webpack configuration.

Example:

```js
module.exports = {
  devServer: {
    proxy: 'http://localhost:8080'
  }
};
```

Conclusion

Understanding the structure and files of a Vue.js project lays a strong foundation for developing a robust Progressive Web App. Each file and folder has a specific purpose, and knowing how they fit together will help you navigate through your project more efficiently. As you continue developing your PWA, you may customize this structure to better suit your project's needs.

4. Creating Your First Vue.js App

4.1 Setting Up Your Development Environment

Before diving into creating your first Vue.js app, it's crucial to ensure your development environment is correctly set up. In this subchapter, we'll go through the necessary software installations and configurations you need to get started.

Software Requirements

To build a Vue.js application, you'll need the following tools:

42. **Node.js and npm**
43. **A Code Editor**
44. **Vue CLI (we will cover this in detail in the next subchapter)**

Node.js and npm

Node.js is a JavaScript runtime that allows you to run JavaScript on the server side, and npm (Node Package Manager) is used for managing libraries and dependencies.

To install Node.js and npm, follow these steps:

45. Visit the official Node.js website at https://nodejs.org/.
46. Download the latest stable version for your operating system.
47. Run the installer and follow the setup instructions.

To verify the installation, open your terminal and run:

```
node -v
```

This command checks the installed Node.js version.

Next, check if npm was installed correctly by running:

```
npm -v
```

This command will display the installed npm version.

A Code Editor

A good code editor will significantly improve your development experience. Popular choices include:

- Visual Studio Code: https://code.visualstudio.com/
- Sublime Text: https://www.sublimetext.com/
- Atom: https://atom.io/

Download and install a code editor of your choice.

Configuring Your Code Editor

After installing your preferred code editor, you should configure it for a Vue.js project. Here, we'll use Visual Studio Code for demonstration.

Visual Studio Code Extensions

48. **Vetur**: Provides syntax-highlighting and IntelliSense for Vue.js.

    To install Vetur:

    - Open Visual Studio Code.
    - Go to the Extensions panel by clicking the square icon on the sidebar or pressing `Ctrl+Shift+X`.
    - Search for "Vetur" and click "Install".

49. **ESLint**: Ensures code quality by detecting errors and enforcing coding standards.

    To install ESLint:

    - Follow the same steps as above and search for "ESLint".

- Click "Install".

Additional Configuration

You might also want to configure some settings in your code editor:

50. **Format on Save**

    Enable automatic code formatting on save by adding the following settings in Visual Studio Code's `settings.json` file:

    ```
    {
      "editor.formatOnSave": true,
      "vetur.format.options.tabSize": 2,
      "vetur.format.options.useTabs": false,
      "eslint.autoFixOnSave": true
    }
    ```

Terminal Configuration

A good terminal can enhance your productivity. The default terminal on your operating system will work, but you might prefer an upgraded version:

- **iTerm2** (MacOS): https://iterm2.com/
- **Windows Terminal** (Windows): https://aka.ms/terminal

Summary

You now have Node.js, npm, and a code editor configured to support Vue.js development. In the next section, we'll delve into installing Vue CLI, which will streamline the setup and management of your Vue.js projects. With your development environment primed, you are now ready to start creating your first Vue.js app.

4.2 Installing Vue CLI

A streamlined and effective setup is crucial for building modern web applications. Vue CLI (Command Line Interface) is an essential tool that simplifies the process of starting and managing your Vue.js projects by offering an easy-to-use command line interface. This subchapter will guide you through installing Vue CLI, ensuring you have the foundational tools needed for building your first Vue.js application.

Prerequisites

Before installing Vue CLI, ensure that Node.js and npm (Node Package Manager) are installed on your system. You can verify their installation by running the following commands:

```
node -v
npm -v
```

If you don't have Node.js and npm installed, you can download and install the latest version from the official Node.js website: https://nodejs.org/

Installing Vue CLI

Vue CLI is distributed as an npm package. To install it globally on your system, open your terminal or command prompt and run the following command:

```
npm install -g @vue/cli
```

The -g flag ensures that Vue CLI is installed globally, making the 'vue' command available from any directory on your system.

Verifying the Installation

To confirm that Vue CLI has been installed correctly, you can check the version of Vue CLI by executing:

```
vue --version
```

If the installation was successful, you should see the version number of the Vue CLI displayed in your terminal.

Common Installation Issues

Path Issues

If you encounter a 'command not found' error after installation, it may be due to the npm global bin directory not being in your system's PATH. You can add it manually to your PATH environment variable.

For Unix-based systems (like macOS or Linux), add the following line to your `.bashrc`, `.bash_profile`, or `.zshrc` file:

```
export PATH=$PATH:$(npm config get prefix)/bin
```

For Windows, follow these steps:

51. Open System Properties (Windows + Pause).

52. Click on "Advanced system settings".

53. Click on the "Environment Variables" button.

54. Under "System Variables", select "Path" and click on "Edit".

55. Add the path returned by the following npm command:

```
npm config get prefix
```

Permission Issues

On some systems, installing packages globally might require elevated permissions. If you see permission errors, prepend the installation command with `sudo` on Unix-based systems:

```
sudo npm install -g @vue/cli
```

On Windows, make sure you run the command prompt as an Administrator.

Updating Vue CLI

Keeping your tools up to date is essential for making use of the latest features and bug fixes. To update Vue CLI to the latest version, you can run the following command:

```
npm update -g @vue/cli
```

Summary

In this subchapter, you have learned how to install Vue CLI, an indispensable tool for Vue.js development. With Vue CLI successfully installed, you are now equipped to create and manage Vue.js projects effortlessly. Proceed to the next subchapter, where we will guide you through creating your first Vue.js project using the Vue CLI, setting the stage for building your progressive web app.

4.3 Creating a New Vue.js Project

After setting up your development environment and installing Vue CLI, you are now ready to create your first Vue.js project. This section will guide you through the steps needed to initialize a new Vue.js project using Vue CLI, configure basic options, and understand the structure of your new project.

Initializing a New Vue.js Project

The first step in creating a new Vue.js project is to use the Vue CLI to generate the project scaffolding. Open your terminal or command prompt and run the following command:

```
vue create my-first-vue-app
```

Replace `my-first-vue-app` with the name you wish to give to your project. This command will prompt you to select a preset or manually configure your project.

Choosing Configuration Options

When you run the `vue create` command, you will have the option to either choose the default preset (for a quick setup) or manually select the features you want to include in your project.

For selecting features manually, you will encounter the following prompts:

56. **Please pick a preset:**
    - default ([Vue 2] babel, eslint)
    - Manually select features

57. **Check the features needed for your project:**
    - Babel
    - TypeScript
    - Progressive Web App (PWA) Support
    - Router
    - Vuex
    - CSS Pre-processors
    - Linter / Formatter
    - Unit Testing
    - E2E Testing

Here's an example of how the selection process might look:

```
? Please pick a preset: Manually select features
? Check the features needed for your project: Babel, Router
, Vuex, Linter / Formatter
? Use history mode for router? (Requires proper server setu
p for index fallback in production) Yes
? Pick a linter / formatter config: ESLint with error preve
ntion only
? Pick additional lint features: Lint on save
? Where do you prefer placing config for Babel, ESLint, etc
.? In dedicated config files
? Save this as a preset for future projects? No
```

Understanding the Project Structure

Once the Vue CLI has generated the project structure, you will see a directory named `my-first-vue-app` with the following structure:

```
my-first-vue-app/
├── node_modules/
├── public/
│   ├── favicon.ico
│   └── index.html
├── src/
│   ├── assets/
│   ├── components/
│   │   └── HelloWorld.vue
│   ├── router/
│   │   └── index.js
│   ├── store/
│   │   └── index.js
│   ├── App.vue
│   └── main.js
├── .gitignore
├── babel.config.js
├── package.json
├── README.md
└── vue.config.js
```

Key Files and Directories

- **public/**: Contains static assets such as the favicon and the index.html file.
- **src/**: Contains the main source code of your application.
    - **assets/**: Directory for static assets like images and styles.
    - **components/**: Directory for Vue components.
    - **router/**: Configurations for Vue Router (only if you selected Router during setup).
    - **store/**: Configurations for Vuex (only if you selected Vuex during setup).
    - **App.vue**: The root Vue component.
    - **main.js**: The entry point for your application.
- **Configuration Files**:
    - **.gitignore**: Specifies files and directories to be ignored by Git.

- **babel.config.js**: Babel configuration.
- **vue.config.js**: Vue CLI configuration.
- **package.json**: Project metadata and dependencies.

Running Your New Vue.js Application

To run your new Vue.js application, navigate to the project directory and start the development server:

```
cd my-first-vue-app
npm run serve
```

After executing the command, you should see output similar to the following:

```
 DONE  Compiled successfully in 4215ms
8:32:27 PM

  App running at:
  - Local:   http://localhost:8080/
  - Network: http://192.168.1.5:8080/
```

Open your browser and navigate to `http://localhost:8080/` to see your newly created Vue.js application.

In the next section, we will explore your app in detail, examining how the files and directories are interrelated and how you can customize your new Vue.js project further.

4.4 Running and Exploring Your App

Now that you have successfully created your first Vue.js application, it's time to see it in action! In this section, we will run your app and explore its structure. By the end of this section, you will be familiar with how Vue.js organizes your project and how you can interact with the Vue CLI to manage your development workflow.

Starting the Development Server

To start your Vue.js application, navigate to your project directory if you are not already there:

```
cd your-vue-app
```

Once you are in the project directory, start the local development server with the following command:

```
npm run serve
```

This will start a development server and compile your application. You should see output similar to this:

```
App running at:
- Local:   http://localhost:8080/
- Network: http://192.168.0.101:8080/
```

Open your browser and navigate to `http://localhost:8080/`. You should see the default Vue.js welcome screen, which confirms that your app is running successfully.

Project Structure

Let's take a quick look at the files and folders generated by Vue CLI to understand their purpose:

Main Project Folder:

```
your-vue-app
├── node_modules/
├── public/
├── src/
│   ├── assets/
│   ├── components/
│   ├── App.vue
│   └── main.js
├── .gitignore
├── babel.config.js
├── package.json
├── README.md
└── vue.config.js
```

Key Files and Directories:

- **node_modules/**: Contains all the npm packages installed for your project.
- **public/**: This directory includes index.html, which is the entry point of your application.
- **src/**: The source folder where the main application's code resides.
    - **assets/**: A folder for static assets like images and stylesheets.
    - **components/**: A folder for Vue components.
    - **App.vue**: Root component for your application.
    - **main.js**: The entry JavaScript file that bootstraps your Vue app.
- **.gitignore**: Specifies which files and directories to ignore in version control.

- **babel.config.js**: Configuration file for Babel, which is used for JavaScript transpiling.
- **package.json**: Contains metadata about the project, including dependencies and scripts.
- **README.md**: Auto-generated README file with basic information about your project.
- **vue.config.js**: Configuration file for Vue CLI optional settings.

Exploring the Default Vue Component

The `App.vue` file is the root component of your Vue application. Open `src/App.vue` to see the code:

```
<template>
  <div id="app">
    <img alt="Vue logo" src="./assets/logo.png">
    <HelloWorld msg="Welcome to Your Vue.js App"/>
  </div>
</template>

<script>
import HelloWorld from './components/HelloWorld.vue'

export default {
  name: 'App',
  components: {
    HelloWorld
  }
}
</script>

<style>
#app {
  font-family: Avenir, Helvetica, Arial, sans-serif;
  -webkit-font-smoothing: antialiased;
  -moz-osx-font-smoothing: grayscale;
  text-align: center;
  color: #2c3e50;
  margin-top: 60px;
}
</style>
```

Modifying Your App

Let's make a simple modification to see changes in action:

> 58. Open `src/components/HelloWorld.vue`.
> 59. Change the `<h1>` tag to display a different message.

Here's an example:

```
<template>
  <div class="hello">
    <h1>My First Vue.js App</h1>
    <p>{{ msg }}</p>
  </div>
</template>

<script>
export default {
  name: 'HelloWorld',
  props: {
    msg: String
  }
}
</script>

<style scoped>
h1, h2 {
  font-weight: normal;
}
ul {
  list-style-type: none;
  padding: 0;
}
a {
  color: #42b983;
}
</style>
```

Save the file and go back to your browser. You should see the new message "My First Vue.js App" displayed.

Conclusion

In this section, you learned how to start your Vue.js application using the Vue CLI, explored the project structure, and made simple modifications to your app. Now, you are ready to dive deeper into building more complex applications and implementing Progressive Web App features.

5. Implementing Progressive Web App Features

5.1 Introduction to Service Workers

Service workers are a pivotal technology for building Progressive Web Apps (PWAs). They act as a proxy server that sits between your web application and the network, allowing you to intercept network requests, cache resources, and deliver push notifications even when the user is offline. This subchapter aims to provide a thorough understanding of service workers and how to use them effectively within your Vue.js application.

What is a Service Worker?

A service worker is essentially a JavaScript file that runs in a web browser. It operates independently of your main application thread, which means it doesn't interfere with the user interface. The primary functionalities of a service worker include:

- **Intercepting and handling network requests**: Making it possible to serve asset files and API calls from the cache.
- **Background data synchronization**: Ensuring data is synced in the background even when the app isn't in the foreground.
- **Push notifications**: Allowing the app to receive and display notifications even when it isn't currently open.

Registering a Service Worker

To use a service worker, you must first register it. This is typically done in your main JavaScript file. The following example demonstrates how to register a service worker in a Vue.js application.

```
if ('serviceWorker' in navigator) {
  navigator.serviceWorker.register('/service-worker.js')
  .then(registration => {
    console.log('Service Worker registered with scope:', re
gistration.scope);
  }).catch(error => {
    console.log('Service Worker registration failed:', erro
r);
  });
} else {
  console.log('Service Workers are not supported by this br
owser.');
}
```

Life Cycle of a Service Worker

Service workers follow a well-defined lifecycle, consisting of the following phases:

60. **Installation**: During this phase, the service worker is downloaded and installed. You typically use this event to cache static assets.

    ```
    self.addEventListener('install', event => {
      event.waitUntil(
        caches.open('my-cache').then(cache => {
          return cache.addAll([
            '/',
            '/index.html',
            '/styles.css',
            '/script.js'
          ]);
        })
      );
    });
    ```

61. **Activation**: After the installation, the service worker is activated. This phase is typically used to clean up old caches.

    ```
    self.addEventListener('activate', event => {
      event.waitUntil(
        caches.keys().then(cacheNames => {
          return Promise.all(
    ```

```
            cacheNames.filter(cacheName => {
              return cacheName !== 'my-cache';
            }).map(cacheName => {
              return caches.delete(cacheName);
            })
          );
        })
      );
    });
```

62. **Fetch**: Once active, the service worker can intercept network requests. This phase is where you can control caching strategies.

```
    self.addEventListener('fetch', event => {
      event.respondWith(
        caches.match(event.request).then(response => {
          return response || fetch(event.request);
        })
      );
    });
```

Debugging Service Workers

While service workers are powerful, they can be tricky to debug due to their asynchronous nature and separate threading. Modern browsers provide tools to help with this. In Chrome, for example, you can go to chrome://serviceworker-internals to get detailed information. Additionally, the Application panel in Chrome DevTools provides comprehensive debugging options, including:

- Viewing registered service workers
- Unregistering service workers
- Simulating offline mode
- Inspecting caches

Service Worker Gotchas

Despite their benefits, service workers come with their own set of challenges:

63. **Scope Limitations**: Service workers are scoped to the directory in which they are registered. Therefore, registering a service worker located at `/service-worker.js` would give it control over all the pages in the root and its subdirectories.

64. **HTTPS Requirement**: Service workers only work on secure origins (over HTTPS) due to their powerful features and potential side effects.

65. **Lifecycle Complexity**: The lifecycle events can sometimes lead to unexpected behavior if not managed correctly, especially during the installation and activation stages.

Summary

Service workers are a cornerstone of Progressive Web Apps, offering capabilities like offline support, background sync, and push notifications. By understanding how to register, activate, and fetch resources with service workers, you can significantly improve the performance and reliability of your Vue.js application.

In the next section, we'll dive deeper into adding offline support using service workers, ensuring your application remains robust and user-friendly even in the absence of an internet connection.

5.2 Adding Offline Support

Adding offline support to your Progressive Web App (PWA) is a crucial step in ensuring that your app can function effectively even when the user doesn't have an internet connection. This involves leveraging service workers to cache essential files, so they can be loaded from the local cache when the network is unavailable. In this subchapter, we'll guide you through the process of adding offline support to your Vue.js application.

Setting Up Service Worker for Offline Caching

Before we start adding offline support, ensure that you have a service worker set up. If you haven't already created a service worker, refer to subchapter 5.1 Introduction to Service Workers.

Precaching Static Assets

Precache static assets such as HTML, JS, CSS, and images so that they are available offline. Here's a basic example using the Workbox library, which simplifies service worker development.

First, install the Workbox library:

```
npm install workbox-cli --save-dev
```

Next, create a `workbox-config.js` file in the root of your project to specify what files to cache:

```
module.exports = {
  "globDirectory": "dist/",
  "globPatterns": [
    "**/*.{html,json,js,css,png,jpg}"
  ],
  "swDest": "dist/service-worker.js",
  "swSrc": "src/service-worker.js"
};
```

Update your `package.json` to add a build step for Workbox:

```
"scripts": {
  "build:workbox": "workbox generateSW workbox-config.js",
  "build": "vue-cli-service build && npm run build:workbox"
}
```

Create a `src/service-worker.js` file to handle the caching logic:

```
import { precacheAndRoute } from 'workbox-precaching';

precacheAndRoute(self.__WB_MANIFEST);
```

This script uses `precacheAndRoute` to precache and serve static files. Now, run the build command:

```
npm run build
```

Dynamic Caching of API Requests

Besides precaching, you'll likely need to cache API requests to ensure your app can retrieve data when offline. Update your `src/service-worker.js` to include dynamic caching:

```js
import { registerRoute } from 'workbox-routing';
import { NetworkFirst } from 'workbox-strategies';

// Cache API responses
registerRoute(
  ({url}) => url.origin === 'https://your.api.url',
  new NetworkFirst({
    cacheName: 'api-cache',
    plugins: [
      {
        cacheWillUpdate: async ({request, response, event}) => {
          if (response.status === 200) {
            return response;
          }
          return null;
        },
      },
    ],
  })
);
```

Replace `https://your.api.url` with your actual API URL. The `NetworkFirst` strategy attempts to fetch data from the network first and then falls back to the cache if the network is unavailable.

Handling App Shell

To provide a seamless offline experience, your app should cache the app shell—essentially the core HTML, CSS, and JavaScript files required to render the user interface. This ensures that your PWA can load instantly, even if network conditions are poor.

Modify your `src/service-worker.js` to handle app shell caching:

```
import { CacheFirst } from 'workbox-strategies';

registerRoute(
  ({request}) => request.mode === 'navigate',
  new CacheFirst({
    cacheName: 'app-shell',
    plugins: [
      {
        cacheWillUpdate: async ({request, response, event}) => {
          if (response && response.status === 200 && request.headers.get('content-type').includes('text/html')) {
            return response;
          }
          return null;
        },
      },
    ],
  })
);
```

Testing Offline Support

After configuring your service worker for offline support, it's essential to test it. Use Chrome DevTools to simulate offline conditions:

66. Open your app in Chrome.
67. Press `F12` to open DevTools.
68. Go to the `Application` tab.
69. In the `Service Workers` section, check "Offline."

Now, try navigating your app. If correctly implemented, it should load the app shell and any cached data seamlessly.

Handling Stale Content

Even though you are caching assets and API responses, you might want to periodically update the content to keep your app fresh. Implement a cache update strategy, such as "stale-while-revalidate," using Workbox:

```
import { StaleWhileRevalidate } from 'workbox-strategies';

registerRoute(
  ({url}) => url.origin === 'https://your.api.url',
  new StaleWhileRevalidate({
    cacheName: 'dynamic-cache',
  })
);
```

This strategy serves cached content first and then updates the cache with the latest data from the network.

Conclusion

Adding offline support can significantly improve the user experience of your PWA by ensuring it remains functional even without an internet connection. By leveraging service workers and caching strategies, you can make critical resources available offline and handle dynamic content effectively. In the next subchapter, we will explore implementing push notifications to keep users engaged even when they are not actively using your application.

5.3 Implementing Push Notifications

Push notifications are a powerful feature of Progressive Web Apps (PWAs). They allow you to re-engage users by sending timely, relevant messages even when the web app is not in use. This subchapter will guide you through the steps of implementing push notifications in your Vue.js-based PWA.

Understanding Push Notifications

Push notifications are initiated by the server and received by the client via a service worker. They consist of two main parts: 1. **The Push API**: Responsible for subscribing the client to push notifications. 2. **The Notification API**: Used to display notifications to the user.

Setting Up Push Notifications

To implement push notifications in your Vue.js PWA, follow these steps:

Requesting User Permission

First, you need to request permission from the user to send push notifications. You can use the Notification API to ask for this permission:

```
if ('Notification' in window && 'serviceWorker' in navigator) {
  Notification.requestPermission(status => {
    console.log('Notification permission status:', status);
  });
} else {
  console.log('Push messaging is not supported.');
}
```

Registering the Service Worker

Register the service worker to handle incoming push events:

```
if ('serviceWorker' in navigator) {
  navigator.serviceWorker.register('/service-worker.js')
    .then(function(registration) {
      console.log('Service Worker registered with scope:', registration.scope);
    }).catch(function(error) {
      console.error('Service Worker registration failed:', error);
    });
}
```

Ensure your service worker script (`/service-worker.js`) handles the push event:

```
self.addEventListener('push', function(event) {
  const options = {
    body: event.data.text(),
    icon: '/images/notification-icon.png',
    badge: '/images/notification-badge.png'
  };

  event.waitUntil(
    self.registration.showNotification('My Vue.js PWA', options)
  );
});
```

Subscribing to Push Notifications

To receive push notifications, the client must subscribe to a push service. This example uses the **VAPID** (Voluntary Application Server Identification for Web Push) keys for server authentication.

Generating VAPID Keys

Generate VAPID keys using a tool like `web-push`:

```
npm install -g web-push
web-push generate-vapid-keys
```

This will output a public and private key pair. Save these keys for use in both the client and server implementations.

Subscribing the Client

Subscribe the client to a push service using the VAPID public key:

```
navigator.serviceWorker.ready.then(function(registration) {
  const vapidPublicKey = 'YOUR_PUBLIC_VAPID_KEY_HERE';
  const convertedVapidKey = urlBase64ToUint8Array(vapidPublicKey);

  registration.pushManager.subscribe({
    userVisibleOnly: true,
    applicationServerKey: convertedVapidKey
  }).then(function(subscription) {
    console.log('Successfully subscribed to push notifications:', subscription);
    // Send subscription details to the server
    sendSubscriptionToServer(subscription);
  }).catch(function(error) {
    console.error('Failed to subscribe to push notifications:', error);
  });
});

function urlBase64ToUint8Array(base64String) {
  const padding = '='.repeat((4 - base64String.length % 4) % 4);
  const base64 = (base64String + padding)
    .replace(/-/g, '+')
    .replace(/_/g, '/');

  const rawData = window.atob(base64);
  const outputArray = new Uint8Array(rawData.length);

  for (let i = 0; i < rawData.length; ++i) {
    outputArray[i] = rawData.charCodeAt(i);
  }
  return outputArray;
}
```

Sending Notifications from the Server

The server sends push notifications to the subscribed clients. Here's an example using **Node.js** and **web-push** to send a notification:

Setting Up the Server

Install web-push:

```
npm install web-push
```

Sending a Push Message

Create a script to send notifications:

```
const webPush = require('web-push');

const vapidKeys = {
  publicKey: 'YOUR_PUBLIC_VAPID_KEY_HERE',
  privateKey: 'YOUR_PRIVATE_VAPID_KEY_HERE',
};

webPush.setVapidDetails(
  'mailto:your-email@example.com',
  vapidKeys.publicKey,
  vapidKeys.privateKey
);

const subscription = { // replace this with the subscription object you got from client
  endpoint: 'https://fcm.googleapis.com/fcm/send/eXXXXXXXXXXXX',
  keys: {
    auth: 'YOUR_AUTH_KEY',
    p256dh: 'YOUR_P256DH_KEY'
  }
};

const payload = 'Your custom message text here';

webPush.sendNotification(subscription, payload)
  .then(response => console.log('Push notification sent:', response))
  .catch(error => console.error('Error sending push notification:', error));
```

Handling Notifications in the Service Worker

Finally, handle the notification click in the service worker:

```
self.addEventListener('notificationclick', function(event) {
  event.notification.close();

  event.waitUntil(
    clients.openWindow('https://your-pwa-url.com')
  );
});
```

Conclusion

Push notifications are an effective way to keep users engaged with your application. By following the steps outlined in this subchapter, you can implement push notifications in your Vue.js PWA and provide a better user experience. Remember to handle user permissions carefully and ensure that your service worker is correctly set up to display notifications and handle their interactions.

5.4 Enhancing Performance and Security

In this section, we'll explore strategies for improving the performance and security of your Progressive Web App (PWA). Enhancing these aspects of your app is crucial for providing a smooth, reliable, and safe user experience.

Optimizing Performance

Improving the performance of your PWA ensures fast load times, smooth interactions, and an overall responsive feel. Here are several techniques to achieve this:

Code Splitting

Code splitting can improve load times by breaking down your JavaScript into smaller chunks that are loaded on demand. This is particularly useful for large applications.

Here's how you can implement code splitting in a Vue.js app:

```js
import Vue from 'vue';
import Router from 'vue-router';

Vue.use(Router);

const Home = () => import('./components/Home.vue');
const About = () => import('./components/About.vue');

const router = new Router({
  routes: [
    {
      path: '/',
      name: 'Home',
      component: Home,
    },
    {
      path: '/about',
      name: 'About',
      component: About,
    },
  ],
});

export default router;
```

Lazy Loading Components

Lazy loading components ensures that only the necessary components are loaded initially, deferring the loading of other components until needed.

Example of lazy loading a component in Vue.js:

```vue
<template>
  <div>
    <button @click="showComponent = true">Load Component</button>
    <Suspense v-if="showComponent">
      <template #default>
        <AsyncComponent />
      </template>
      <template #fallback>
        <div>Loading...</div>
      </template>
    </Suspense>
  </div>
</template>

<script>
export default {
  data() {
    return {
      showComponent: false,
    };
  },
  components: {
    AsyncComponent: () => import('./components/AsyncComponent.vue'),
  },
};
</script>
```

Implementing Client-side Caching

Caching assets on the client-side can drastically decrease load times for repeat visits. This can be done using the Service Worker API.

Example of adding client-side caching using a service worker:

```
self.addEventListener('install', event => {
  event.waitUntil(
    caches.open('my-cache')
      .then(cache => {
        return cache.addAll([
          '/index.html',
          '/styles.css',
          '/script.js',
        ]);
      })
  );
});

self.addEventListener('fetch', event => {
  event.respondWith(
    caches.match(event.request)
      .then(response => {
        return response || fetch(event.request);
      })
  );
});
```

Enhancing Security

Security in PWAs is paramount for protecting user data and maintaining trust. Here are some methods to enhance the security of your PWA:

Enforcing HTTPS

All Progressive Web Apps must be served over HTTPS to ensure data integrity and security. Modern browsers enforce this as a requirement for certain PWA features, like service workers.

Ensure your server configuration enforces HTTPS:

```
server {
    listen 80;
    server_name yourdomain.com www.yourdomain.com;
    return 301 https://$server_name$request_uri;
}
server {
    listen 443 ssl;
    server_name yourdomain.com www.yourdomain.com;

    ssl_certificate /path/to/ssl_certificate.crt;
    ssl_certificate_key /path/to/ssl_certificate_key.key;

    location / {
        proxy_pass http://localhost:3000;
    }
}
```

Content Security Policy (CSP)

A Content Security Policy (CSP) helps to reduce the risk of cross-site scripting (XSS) attacks by specifying which content sources are trusted.

Implementing CSP in your app:

```
<meta http-equiv="Content-Security-Policy" content="default-src 'self'; style-src 'self' https://fonts.googleapis.com; script-src 'self' https://apis.google.com">
```

Secure Storage

For storing sensitive data, always use secure storage solutions like the Web Cryptography API.

Example of encrypting data in secure storage:

```
async function encryptData(data) {
  const encoder = new TextEncoder();
  const encodedData = encoder.encode(data);
  const key = await crypto.subtle.generateKey(
    { name: 'AES-GCM', length: 256 },
    true,
    ['encrypt', 'decrypt']
  );
  const iv = window.crypto.getRandomValues(new Uint8Array(12));
  const encryptedData = await crypto.subtle.encrypt(
    { name: 'AES-GCM', iv: iv },
    key,
    encodedData
  );
  return { encryptedData, key, iv };
}
```

Regularly Updating Dependencies

Outdated dependencies can be an entry point for vulnerabilities. Regularly updating your dependencies ensures that you are protected against known security issues.

Keep dependencies up-to-date using tools like npm or yarn:

```
npm update
```

By applying these performance and security enhancements, your Progressive Web App will offer a better user experience and safeguard user data effectively.

6. Working with Vue.js Components

6.1 Introduction to Vue.js Components

Vue.js is a powerful and flexible JavaScript framework for building user interfaces, particularly single-page applications (SPAs). A foundational concept in Vue.js is the component system, which is a key feature for building scalable and maintainable applications. In this subchapter, we will explore what Vue.js components are, why they are useful, and how to start working with them.

What are Vue.js Components?

In Vue.js, a component is a reusable piece of code that controls a part of the user interface. Components in Vue.js are akin to custom HTML elements, allowing you to use them declaratively in your templates. Each component encapsulates its own structure (HTML), style (CSS), and behavior (JavaScript), promoting separation of concerns and reusability.

Why Use Components?

- **Reusability**: Components enable you to reuse code across different parts of your application, reducing duplication and improving consistency.
- **Encapsulation**: Components encapsulate their own logic and styling, reducing the risk of side effects in other parts of the application.
- **Maintainability**: By breaking down the user interface into smaller, manageable pieces, components make the application easier to understand, test, and maintain.
- **Separation of Concerns**: Components promote a clear separation between the structure, styling, and behavior of the application.

Basic Structure of a Vue.js Component

A typical Vue.js component consists of three main sections: - **Template**: Defines the HTML structure. - **Script**: Contains the JavaScript logic. - **Style**: Contains the CSS for the component.

Here is a basic example of a Vue.js component:

```
<template>
  <div class="hello-world">
    <h1>{{ message }}</h1>
  </div>
</template>

<script>
export default {
  name: 'HelloWorld',
  data() {
    return {
      message: 'Hello, World!'
    };
  }
};
</script>

<style scoped>
.hello-world {
  text-align: center;
}
</style>
```

Registering Components

Components can be registered in two ways: locally and globally.

Local Registration: Locally registered components are only available in the parent component where they are registered.

```
import HelloWorld from './HelloWorld.vue';

export default {
  components: {
    HelloWorld
  }
};
```

Global Registration: Globally registered components can be used in any component throughout the application.

```
import Vue from 'vue';
import HelloWorld from './HelloWorld.vue';

Vue.component('HelloWorld', HelloWorld);
```

Using Components in Templates

Once a component is registered, you can use it in your templates just like a regular HTML element.

Example of Using a Component:

```
<template>
  <div id="app">
    <HelloWorld />
  </div>
</template>

<script>
import HelloWorld from './components/HelloWorld.vue';

export default {
  name: 'App',
  components: {
    HelloWorld
  }
};
</script>
```

Conclusion

Components are the building blocks of Vue.js applications. They help in organizing code, improving reusability, and promoting separation of concerns. Understanding how to create, register, and use components is essential for any Vue.js developer. In the next sections, we will dive deeper into creating components, managing their communication, and exploring advanced component patterns.

6.2 Creating Your First Component

In this section, we will dive into building your first Vue.js component. Components are the building blocks of Vue.js applications. They encapsulate reusable pieces of the user interface, making it easier to manage and scale your app. Let's walk through the steps to create a simple Vue.js component.

Setting Up the Component

First, let's create a new Vue component. Components can be defined globally or locally.

Globally Registered Component:

```
// main.js
import Vue from 'vue';
import App from './App.vue';

Vue.component('my-component', {
  template: '<div>Hello from My Component!</div>'
});

new Vue({
  render: h => h(App),
}).$mount('#app');
```

In this example, we register a global component called my-component. This component can now be used anywhere in our Vue instance.

Locally Registered Component:

To register a component locally within a parent component, follow these steps:

```
// MyComponent.vue
<template>
  <div>Hello from My Component!</div>
</template>

<script>
export default {
  name: 'MyComponent'
};
</script>

// ParentComponent.vue
<template>
  <div>
    <MyComponent />
  </div>
</template>

<script>
import MyComponent from './MyComponent.vue';

export default {
  components: {
    MyComponent
  }
};
</script>
```

By importing and registering the `MyComponent` locally within `ParentComponent`, you encapsulate it within the parent's scope.

Using the Component

With the component registered, you can now use it in your templates. For the globally registered component, open your `App.vue` file and include it:

```
<template>
  <div id="app">
    <my-component></my-component>
  </div>
</template>

<script>
export default {
  name: 'App'
};
</script>
```

For the locally registered component, it can be used directly within the parent's template as shown earlier:

```
<template>
  <div>
    <MyComponent></MyComponent>
  </div>
</template>
```

Adding Data and Methods

Let's enhance our component by adding data properties and methods.

```
// MyComponent.vue
<template>
  <div>
    <p>{{ message }}</p>
    <button @click="updateMessage">Click me</button>
  </div>
</template>

<script>
export default {
  data() {
    return {
      message: 'Hello from My Component!'
    };
  },
  methods: {
    updateMessage() {
      this.message = 'You clicked the button!';
    }
  }
};
</script>
```

In this example, the `MyComponent` has a `message` property in its data object and an `updateMessage` method. When the button is clicked, the `updateMessage` method updates the `message` property.

Styling the Component

Vue components can include scoped styles to ensure that styles don't leak out and affect other parts of your app.

```vue
// MyComponent.vue
<template>
  <div class="my-component">
    <p>{{ message }}</p>
    <button @click="updateMessage">Click me</button>
  </div>
</template>

<script>
export default {
  data() {
    return {
      message: 'Hello from My Component!'
    };
  },
  methods: {
    updateMessage() {
      this.message = 'You clicked the button!';
    }
  }
};
</script>

<style scoped>
.my-component {
  border: 1px solid #ddd;
  padding: 10px;
  border-radius: 4px;
}

.my-component p {
  color: #333;
}

.my-component button {
  background-color: #42b983;
  color: #fff;
  border: none;
  padding: 10px;
  cursor: pointer;
}

.my-component button:hover {
  background-color: #358a6e;
}
</style>
```

In this example, the styles defined within the `<style scoped>` tag are scoped to `MyComponent`, ensuring that they don't affect other parts of the application.

This is the basic process of creating and using a Vue component. As you progress, you will find that components can become more sophisticated, allowing for slots, props, custom events, mixins, and more to achieve dynamic and reusable UI elements. In the next sections, we'll explore component communication and advanced patterns to further enhance your Vue.js applications.

6.3 Component Communication

Effective communication between components in Vue.js is a fundamental aspect of building scalable and maintainable applications. In this subchapter, we will explore the methods and patterns used to enable component communication in Vue.js. We'll cover parent-to-child, child-to-parent, and sibling component interactions using props, events, and Vue's event bus.

Parent-to-Child Communication with Props

The simplest form of communication in Vue.js is passing data from a parent component to a child component using props. Props are custom attributes you can register on a child component. When a value is passed to a prop, it becomes a reactive property of that component.

Example

Here's a basic example where a parent component passes a message to a child component using props.

ParentComponent.vue:

```vue
<template>
  <div>
    <h1>Parent Component</h1>
    <ChildComponent :message="parentMessage" />
  </div>
</template>

<script>
import ChildComponent from './ChildComponent.vue';

export default {
  components: {
    ChildComponent
  },
  data() {
    return {
      parentMessage: 'Hello from Parent Component!'
    };
  }
};
</script>
```

ChildComponent.vue:

```vue
<template>
  <div>
    <p>{{ message }}</p>
  </div>
</template>

<script>
export default {
  props: {
    message: {
      type: String,
      required: true
    }
  }
};
</script>
```

Child-to-Parent Communication with Custom Events

When a child component needs to send data to a parent component, it can emit a custom event. The parent component can then listen for this event and take appropriate action.

Example

In this example, the child component emits an event when a button is clicked, and the parent component listens for this event.

ChildComponent.vue:

```
<template>
  <div>
    <button @click="notifyParent">Click Me</button>
  </div>
</template>

<script>
export default {
  methods: {
    notifyParent() {
      this.$emit('childClicked', 'Data from Child Component');
    }
  }
};
</script>
```

ParentComponent.vue:

```vue
<template>
  <div>
    <h1>Parent Component</h1>
    <ChildComponent @childClicked="handleChildClick" />
  </div>
</template>

<script>
import ChildComponent from './ChildComponent.vue';

export default {
  components: {
    ChildComponent
  },
  methods: {
    handleChildClick(data) {
      console.log('Event received from child:', data);
    }
  }
};
</script>
```

Sibling Communication Through Event Bus

For sibling components to communicate, you can use a centralized event bus. An event bus is just a Vue instance that facilitates the event system's use for non-parent-child components.

Example

Here's how you can set up an event bus for siblings:

EventBus.js:

```js
import Vue from 'vue';
export const EventBus = new Vue();
```

SiblingOne.vue:

```vue
<template>
  <div>
    <button @click="sendMessage">Send Message to Sibling</button>
  </div>
</template>

<script>
import { EventBus } from './EventBus.js';

export default {
  methods: {
    sendMessage() {
      EventBus.$emit('messageReceived', 'Hello from Sibling One');
    }
  }
};
</script>
```

SiblingTwo.vue:

```vue
<template>
  <div>
    <p>{{ message }}</p>
  </div>
</template>

<script>
import { EventBus } from './EventBus.js';

export default {
  data() {
    return {
      message: ''
    };
  },
  created() {
    EventBus.$on('messageReceived', (msg) => {
      this.message = msg;
    });
  }
};
</script>
```

Advanced Communication Patterns

While props, events, and an event bus are straightforward methods for component communication, Vue.js also provides more advanced patterns like Vuex for managing state across your application. Vuex will be covered in detail in Chapter 7: Managing State with Vuex.

Summary

In this subchapter, we covered the essential methods for component communication in Vue.js. You have learned how to: 1. Pass data from parent to child using props. 2. Emit custom events from child to parent. 3. Use an event bus for sibling communication.

Understanding these patterns will help you create more dynamic and interactive applications. Up next, we will explore advanced component patterns to enhance your Vue.js skills.

6.4 Advanced Component Patterns

As you grow more comfortable with Vue.js, you will encounter scenarios requiring more sophisticated component patterns. This subchapter explores advanced techniques for making your Vue.js components more dynamic, maintainable, and reusable. We will cover dynamic components, higher-order components, render functions, and scoped slots.

Dynamic Components

Dynamic components allow you to switch between components at runtime using the `<component>` element and the `is` attribute. This is useful for conditionally rendering components or creating complex user interfaces.

```
<template>
  <div>
    <button @click="currentComponent = 'ComponentA'">Show C
omponent A</button>
    <button @click="currentComponent = 'ComponentB'">Show C
omponent B</button>

    <component :is="currentComponent"></component>
  </div>
</template>

<script>
import ComponentA from './ComponentA.vue';
import ComponentB from './ComponentB.vue';

export default {
  data() {
    return {
      currentComponent: 'ComponentA'
    };
  },
  components: {
    ComponentA,
    ComponentB
  }
};
</script>
```

Higher-Order Components

Higher-Order Components (HOCs) are functions that take a component and return a new component, enhancing the existing component with new functionality. They are similar to higher-order functions in JavaScript.

```js
// HOC function
function withLogging(WrappedComponent) {
  return {
    name: `WithLogging(${WrappedComponent.name})`,
    mounted() {
      console.log(`Component ${WrappedComponent.name} Mounted.`);
    },
    render(h) {
      return h(WrappedComponent);
    }
  };
}

// Using HOC
import MyComponent from './MyComponent.vue';

const MyComponentWithLogging = withLogging(MyComponent);

export default {
  components: {
    MyComponentWithLogging
  }
};
```

Render Functions

Render functions provide an alternative to templates and allow more flexibility. They give you programmatic control over the rendering process and can be useful for dynamic generation of elements.

```js
export default {
  render(h) {
    return h('div', [
      h('h1', 'Hello Render Functions!'),
      h('p', 'This is a paragraph.')
    ]);
  }
};
```

Scoped Slots

Scoped slots allow you to pass data from a child component back to its parent through a slot. This pattern is useful for flexible component compositions where the parent controls parts of the child's content.

```
<!-- Parent Component -->
<template>
  <ChildComponent>
    <template v-slot:default="slotProps">
      <p>Hello, {{ slotProps.message }}</p>
    </template>
  </ChildComponent>
</template>

<script>
import ChildComponent from './ChildComponent.vue';

export default {
  components: {
    ChildComponent
  }
};
</script>

<!-- Child Component -->
<template>
  <slot :message="message"></slot>
</template>

<script>
export default {
  data() {
    return {
      message: 'Scoped Slots are powerful!'
    };
  }
};
</script>
```

Mixins

Mixins allow you to encapsulate reusable code and share functionality across multiple components. They can define any combination of component options to be merged into the component using the mixin.

```js
// Mixin file (loggerMixin.js)
export const loggerMixin = {
  created() {
    this.logHello();
  },
  methods: {
    logHello() {
      console.log('Hello from Mixin!');
    }
  }
};

// Using Mixin in a component
<template>
  <div>Check the console log</div>
</template>

<script>
import { loggerMixin } from './loggerMixin';

export default {
  mixins: [loggerMixin]
};
</script>
```

Custom Directories for Components

To manage large-scale applications, it's prudent to organize your components within directories based on their responsibilities. This not only improves maintainability but also enhances readability.

```
src/
  components/
    base/
      BaseButton.vue
      BaseInput.vue
    Layout/
      Header.vue
      Footer.vue
    views/
      HomePage.vue
      AboutPage.vue
```

In summary, mastering these advanced component patterns will enable you to build robust and flexible Vue.js applications. These techniques will help you write cleaner code and improve the maintainability and scalability of your projects. Integrating these patterns effectively will significantly enhance your development expertise in building Progressive Web Apps with Vue.js.

7. Managing State with Vuex

7.1 Introduction to Vuex

When building modern Progressive Web Apps (PWAs) with Vue.js, managing state efficiently is crucial for maintaining a seamless user experience. As your application scales, keeping track of the state across various components can become complex. Vuex, Vue.js's official state management library, provides a robust solution to this problem.

Vuex is inspired by Flux, the application architecture used by Facebook, and follows the same principles. It allows for managing the state of your app in a centralized store, ensuring that the state is predictable and easier to debug. This subchapter will introduce you to the core concepts of Vuex, how it integrates with Vue.js, and why it's the go-to choice for Vue developers when it comes to state management.

What is Vuex?

Vuex is a state management pattern + library for Vue.js applications. It serves as a centralized store for all components in an application, with rules ensuring that the state can only be mutated in a predictable fashion. Vuex integrates tightly with Vue.js's reactivity system, making state changes efficient and easy to trace.

Why Use Vuex?

In a basic Vue.js application, component data (state) is often maintained within the components themselves using the `data` function. While this is manageable for small applications, it quickly becomes unwieldy as the application grows. Some common issues that arise include:

- **Shared State Management**: Keeping track of shared state across multiple components.
- **State Mutation Tracking**: Debugging and understanding where and why state changes occur.
- **Complexity of Prop Drilling**: Passing down state and events through many layers of components.

Vuex resolves these issues by offering a centralized store to manage the state, enabling a more structured and scalable approach to state management.

Key Concepts of Vuex

State

The state in Vuex is a single source of truth, which means the entire state of the application is contained within a single object. This makes the state straightforward to manage and track changes.

```
const store = new Vuex.Store({
  state: {
    count: 0
  }
});
```

Getters

Getters are like computed properties for the state in Vuex. They allow you to define complex state derivations, making them reusable across components.

```
const store = new Vuex.Store({
  state: {
    count: 0
  },
  getters: {
    doubleCount: state => state.count * 2
  }
});
```

Mutations

Mutations are synchronous functions that change the state in Vuex. They can be thought of as setters in Vue.js components but are explicitly committed.

```
const store = new Vuex.Store({
  state: {
    count: 0
  },
  mutations: {
    increment(state) {
      state.count++;
    }
  }
});
```

Actions

Actions are similar to mutations, but they support asynchronous operations. Instead of directly mutating the state, actions commit mutations.

```
const store = new Vuex.Store({
  state: {
    count: 0
  },
  mutations: {
    increment(state) {
      state.count++;
    }
  },
  actions: {
    incrementAsync({ commit }) {
      setTimeout(() => {
        commit('increment');
      }, 1000);
    }
  }
});
```

Modules

For large applications, Vuex allows you to divide the store into modules. Each module can have its own state, mutations, actions, getters, and even nested modules.

```
const moduleA = {
  state: { /* ... */ },
  mutations: { /* ... */ },
  actions: { /* ... */ },
  getters: { /* ... */ }
};

const store = new Vuex.Store({
  modules: {
    a: moduleA
  }
});
```

Setting Up Vuex

To start using Vuex in your Vue.js project, you first need to install it via npm:

```
npm install vuex --save
```

Next, create a Vuex store and integrate it with your Vue instance:

```
import Vue from 'vue';
import Vuex from 'vuex';

Vue.use(Vuex);

const store = new Vuex.Store({
  state: {
    count: 0
  },
  mutations: {
    increment(state) {
      state.count++;
    }
  }
});

new Vue({
  store,
  render: h => h(App)
}).$mount('#app');
```

Conclusion

Vuex is a powerful tool for managing state in Vue.js applications. By centralizing the state in a single, predictable store, Vuex simplifies the complexity of state management, making your code more maintainable and easier to debug. In the following sections, we will dive deeper into the core concepts of Vuex, explore how to manage state using Vuex stores, and cover advanced techniques to leverage Vuex to its fullest potential.

7.2 Core Concepts of Vuex

Vuex is a state management library for Vue.js applications. It centralizes the state in a single source of truth, making it easier to manage and debug state changes. This subchapter delves into the core concepts of Vuex, including the state, getters, mutations, actions, and modules. Understanding these core concepts is crucial for effectively managing state within your Progressive Web App (PWA).

State

The state in Vuex is a single JavaScript object containing all the data your application needs. It acts as the "source of truth" that can be accessed from any component in your application. By centralizing the state, Vuex ensures that all components always get the latest data.

Example:

```js
// store.js
const state = {
  counter: 0,
};
```

To access the state in a component:

```
<template>
  <div>{{ counter }}</div>
</template>

<script>
export default {
  computed: {
    counter() {
      return this.$store.state.counter;
    },
  },
};
</script>
```

Getters

Getters are similar to computed properties in Vue.js but for the Vuex store. They allow you to compute derived state based on the store state. Getters can be useful for filtering or processing data before it's used by a component.

Example:

```
// store.js
const getters = {
  doubledCounter: (state) => {
    return state.counter * 2;
  },
};

// Vuex store
const store = new Vuex.Store({
  state,
  getters,
});
```

To access a getter in a component:

```
<template>
  <div>{{ doubledCounter }}</div>
</template>

<script>
export default {
  computed: {
    doubledCounter() {
      return this.$store.getters.doubledCounter;
    },
  },
};
</script>
```

Mutations

Mutations are the only way to change the state in Vuex. They are synchronous functions that receive the state as the first argument and the payload as the second argument. Mutations are usually committed from components or actions.

Example:

```
// store.js
const mutations = {
  increment(state, payload) {
    state.counter += payload.amount;
  },
};

// Vuex store
const store = new Vuex.Store({
  state,
  mutations,
});
```

To commit a mutation in a component:

```
<template>
  <button @click="increment">Increment</button>
</template>

<script>
export default {
  methods: {
    increment() {
      this.$store.commit('increment', { amount: 1 });
    },
  },
};
</script>
```

Actions

Actions are similar to mutations but they can be asynchronous. They are often used for API calls or other asynchronous operations before committing mutations. Actions receive a context object which contains the state, getters, commit function, and dispatch function.

Example:

```
// store.js
const actions = {
  asyncIncrement({ commit }, payload) {
    setTimeout(() => {
      commit('increment', payload);
    }, 1000);
  },
};

// Vuex store
const store = new Vuex.Store({
  state,
  mutations,
  actions,
});
```

To dispatch an action in a component:

```
<template>
  <button @click="asyncIncrement">Async Increment</button>
</template>

<script>
export default {
  methods: {
    asyncIncrement() {
      this.$store.dispatch('asyncIncrement', { amount: 1 })
;
    },
  },
};
</script>
```

Modules

As your application grows, the Vuex store can become large and difficult to manage. Vuex modules allow you to split the store into smaller, manageable parts. Each module can contain its state, mutations, actions, and getters, and they can be nested.

Example:

```js
// user.js (a Vuex module)
const state = {
  name: 'John Doe',
};

const getters = {
  getName: (state) => state.name,
};

const mutations = {
  setName(state, payload) {
    state.name = payload.name;
  },
};

const actions = {
  updateName({ commit }, payload) {
    commit('setName', payload);
  },
};

export default {
  state,
  getters,
  mutations,
  actions,
};

// store.js
import Vue from 'vue';
import Vuex from 'vuex';
import user from './user';

Vue.use(Vuex);

const store = new Vuex.Store({
  modules: {
    user,
  },
});

export default store;
```

To use the module in a component:

```vue
<template>
  <div>{{ userName }}</div>
</template>

<script>
export default {
  computed: {
    userName() {
      return this.$store.getters['user/getName'];
    },
  },
  methods: {
    changeName() {
      this.$store.dispatch('user/updateName', { name: 'Jane Doe' });
    },
  },
};
</script>
```

Understanding these core concepts will help you leverage the full power of Vuex in your Vue.js applications, providing a predictable and maintainable state management solution.

7.3 Managing State with Vuex Stores

The Vuex store is the central repository for managing state in a Vue.js application. It enables you to easily access and share data across various components of your application while maintaining a single source of truth. In this subchapter, you will learn how to create, configure, and use Vuex stores effectively.

Setting Up a Vuex Store

To set up a Vuex store, you first need to install the Vuex library if you haven't already. You can do this via npm or yarn:

```
npm install vuex --save
```

or

```
yarn add vuex
```

Once installed, create a `store.js` file in your project directory. This file will contain the configuration for your Vuex store.

```
import Vue from 'vue';
import Vuex from 'vuex';

Vue.use(Vuex);

export default new Vuex.Store({
  state: {
    count: 0
  },
  mutations: {
    increment(state) {
      state.count++;
    }
  },
  actions: {
    increment({ commit }) {
      commit('increment');
    }
  },
  getters: {
    doubleCount(state) {
      return state.count * 2;
    }
  }
});
```

Integrating the Store with Your Vue Application

After setting up the Vuex store, you need to inject it into your Vue application. Open your `main.js` file and make the following changes:

```
import Vue from 'vue';
import App from './App.vue';
import store from './store'; // Import Vuex store

new Vue({
  render: h => h(App),
  store // Inject the store into the Vue instance
}).$mount('#app');
```

Accessing State in Components

You can access the state stored in your Vuex store in any component using the `this.$store.state` property. For example:

```
<template>
  <div>
    <p>Count: {{ count }}</p>
    <button @click="increment">Increment</button>
  </div>
</template>

<script>
export default {
  computed: {
    count() {
      return this.$store.state.count;
    }
  },
  methods: {
    increment() {
      this.$store.commit('increment');
    }
  }
};
</script>
```

Using Getters

Getters allow you to compute derived state based on store state. They serve as computed properties for the store. Using the example store configuration, you can access a getter like this:

```
<template>
  <div>
    <p>Double Count: {{ doubleCount }}</p>
  </div>
</template>

<script>
export default {
  computed: {
    doubleCount() {
      return this.$store.getters.doubleCount;
    }
  }
};
</script>
```

Using Actions

Actions are similar to mutations, but instead of mutating the state, they commit mutations. Actions can contain asynchronous operations and are dispatched rather than committed. Here's an example:

```
<template>
  <div>
    <p>Count: {{ count }}</p>
    <button @click="increment">Increment with Action</button>
  </div>
</template>

<script>
export default {
  computed: {
    count() {
      return this.$store.state.count;
    }
  },
  methods: {
    increment() {
      this.$store.dispatch('increment');
    }
  }
};
</script>
```

Namespacing in Vuex Modules

As your application grows, you might want to split your store into separate modules to keep your code organized. Each module can contain its own state, mutations, actions, and getters. Here's an example of how to create a namespaced module:

```js
// store/modules/counter.js
const state = {
  count: 0
};

const mutations = {
  increment(state) {
    state.count++;
  }
};

const actions = {
  increment({ commit }) {
    commit('increment');
  }
};

const getters = {
  doubleCount(state) {
    return state.count * 2;
  }
};

export default {
  namespaced: true,
  state,
  mutations,
  actions,
  getters
};

// store/index.js
import Vue from 'vue';
import Vuex from 'vuex';
import counter from './modules/counter';

Vue.use(Vuex);

export default new Vuex.Store({
  modules: {
    counter
  }
});
```

You can then access the namespaced state, getters, actions, and mutations in the same manner, but by referencing the module namespace:

```
<template>
  <div>
    <p>Count: {{ count }}</p>
    <button @click="increment">Increment</button>
  </div>
</template>

<script>
export default {
  computed: {
    count() {
      return this.$store.state.counter.count;
    },
    doubleCount() {
      return this.$store.getters['counter/doubleCount'];
    }
  },
  methods: {
    increment() {
      this.$store.dispatch('counter/increment');
    }
  }
};
</script>
```

Conclusion

Managing state with Vuex stores is a powerful technique that provides a structured approach to managing data across your Vue.js components. By understanding how to set up and use Vuex stores, access state, use getters and actions, and organize modules, you are well on your way to building robust and maintainable Progressive Web Apps with Vue.js.

7.4 Advanced Vuex Techniques

In this subchapter, we will explore some advanced techniques and patterns for utilizing Vuex in your Vue.js applications. These techniques will help you manage state more effectively and write more maintainable code.

Namespacing Modules

As your application grows, it is essential to organize your Vuex store to avoid naming collisions and to keep the codebase clean. Vuex allows you to namespace your modules.

```js
// store/modules/user.js
const state = {
  userDetails: {},
};

const mutations = {
  SET_USER_DETAILS(state, details) {
    state.userDetails = details;
  },
};

const actions = {
  fetchUserDetails({ commit }) {
    // Assume an API call that returns user data
    const data = { name: 'John Doe', age: 30 };
    commit('SET_USER_DETAILS', data);
  },
};

export default {
  namespaced: true,
  state,
  mutations,
  actions,
};
```

```js
// store/index.js
import Vue from 'vue';
import Vuex from 'vuex';
import user from './modules/user';

Vue.use(Vuex);

export default new Vuex.Store({
  modules: {
    user
  }
});
```

In your components, you can access the namespaced state and actions easily:

```vue
<template>
  <div>
    <p>User Name: {{ userName }}</p>
    <button @click="getUserDetails">Get User Details</button>
  </div>
</template>

<script>
import { mapState, mapActions } from 'vuex';

export default {
  computed: {
    ...mapState('user', {
      userName: state => state.userDetails.name
    })
  },
  methods: {
    ...mapActions('user', ['fetchUserDetails'])
  }
}
</script>
```

Dynamic Module Registration

Vuex allows dynamic registration of modules, useful for growing or dynamically-loaded applications. It's especially helpful in applications with code-splitting.

```
// Dynamically register a module
this.$store.registerModule('user', {
  namespaced: true,
  state: {
    userDetails: {}
  },
  mutations: {
    SET_USER_DETAILS(state, details) {
      state.userDetails = details;
    }
  },
  actions: {
    fetchUserDetails({ commit }) {
      // Assume an API call that returns user data
      const data = { name: 'Jane Doe', age: 25 };
      commit('SET_USER_DETAILS', data);
    }
  }
});
```

To unregister a module:

```
this.$store.unregisterModule('user');
```

Using Plugins

Plugins can extend Vuex's functionalities. For example, persist the Vuex state across page reloads using a plugin.

```js
// store/plugins/persistState.js
const persistState = store => {
  store.subscribe((mutation, state) => {
    localStorage.setItem('store', JSON.stringify(state));
  });

  const savedState = localStorage.getItem('store');
  if (savedState) {
    store.replaceState(JSON.parse(savedState));
  }
};

export default persistState;
// store/index.js
import Vue from 'vue';
import Vuex from 'vuex';
import persistState from './plugins/persistState';

Vue.use(Vuex);

export default new Vuex.Store({
  plugins: [persistState],
  state: {
    /* initial state */
  },
  mutations: {
    /* mutations */
  },
  actions: {
    /* actions */
  }
});
```

Vuex with TypeScript

If your project uses TypeScript, integrating Vuex requires some additional configuration to benefit from type checking and autocompletion.

```typescript
// store/index.ts
import Vue from 'vue';
import Vuex, { StoreOptions } from 'vuex';

Vue.use(Vuex);

interface RootState {
  user: object;
}

const store: StoreOptions<RootState> = {
  state: {
    user: {}
  },
  mutations: {
    SET_USER(state, payload: object) {
      state.user = payload;
    }
  },
  actions: {
    setUser({ commit }, user: object) {
      commit('SET_USER', user);
    }
  }
};

export default new Vuex.Store<RootState>(store);
```

Using Getters for Complex Computations

Getters can be used for complex state derivations, like filtering and mapping state data.

```js
// store/modules/products.js
const state = {
  products: [
    { id: 1, name: 'Apple', category: 'Fruits' },
    { id: 2, name: 'Carrot', category: 'Vegetables' },
    { id: 3, name: 'Banana', category: 'Fruits' }
  ]
};

const getters = {
  fruits: state => state.products.filter(product => product.category === 'Fruits'),
  productNames: state => state.products.map(product => product.name)
};

export default {
  namespaced: true,
  state,
  getters
};
```

Handling Shared State Across Modules

Sometimes, multiple modules need access to a shared state. This can be structured using root state or leveraging getters and actions.

```js
// Root store
export default new Vuex.Store({
  state: {
    globalNotification: ''
  },
  mutations: {
    SET_NOTIFICATION(state, message) {
      state.globalNotification = message;
    }
  },
  actions: {
    triggerNotification({ commit }, message) {
      commit('SET_NOTIFICATION', message);
    }
  },
  modules: {
    // Your other modules here
  }
});
```

In module actions or components:

```js
// Triggering an action from a module
dispatch('triggerNotification', 'New Notification!', { root: true });
```

By leveraging these advanced Vuex techniques, you can manage increasingly complex state scenarios in your progressive web app efficiently and effectively. These tools empower your Vue.js applications to be more scalable and maintainable, ensuring a smoother development experience.

8. Integrating Service Workers

8.1 Understanding Service Workers

Service workers are at the heart of any Progressive Web App (PWA). These powerful scripts run in the background, independently of your web app. They allow you to intercept network requests, cache responses, and provide a reliable offline experience, even if the user is not actively using your app. In this section, we'll explore what service workers are, how they function, and why they are crucial for Progressive Web Applications built with Vue.js.

The Role of Service Workers

A service worker is essentially a script that the browser runs in the background, separate from the web page itself. This allows developers to leverage features that don't need a web page or user interaction. The main capabilities of service workers include:

- **Interception of Network Requests**: Service workers can intercept network requests and decide how to handle them, whether by fetching the resource from the network, serving it from a cache, or even generating a response dynamically.

- **Caching**: With service workers, you can cache important assets, ensuring that your application is accessible even when the user is offline or experiences network issues.

- **Background Synchronization**: Service workers can sync data in the background, allowing users to continue using your app without waiting for data to be sent or received.

- **Push Notifications**: They can handle push notifications, providing a way to engage with users even when the app is not open.

Lifecycle of a Service Worker

A service worker's lifecycle is distinctly different from that of a regular script in a webpage. It works through a series of phases including installation, activation, and running. Understanding these phases is crucial for effective service worker implementation.

Installation

During this phase, the service worker is downloaded and installed. This is where you would typically set up your cache.

```
self.addEventListener('install', event => {
  event.waitUntil(
    caches.open('my-cache').then(cache => {
      return cache.addAll([
        '/index.html',
        '/styles.css',
        '/script.js',
        '/image.jpg',
        'https://example.com/api/data'
      ]);
    })
  );
});
```

Activation

Once the service worker is installed, it moves to the activation phase. Here, you might want to clean up any old caches.

```
self.addEventListener('activate', event => {
  event.waitUntil(
    caches.keys().then(cacheNames => {
      return Promise.all(
        cacheNames.map(cache => {
          if (cache !== 'my-cache') {
            return caches.delete(cache);
          }
        })
      );
    })
  );
});
```

Fetching

One of the most significant capabilities of a service worker is to intercept and handle network requests. This is done during the fetch phase.

```
self.addEventListener('fetch', event => {
  event.respondWith(
    caches.match(event.request).then(response => {
      return response || fetch(event.request).then(response => {
        return caches.open('my-cache').then(cache => {
          cache.put(event.request.url, response.clone());
          return response;
        });
      });
    }).catch(() => {
      return caches.match('/offline.html');
    })
  );
});
```

Browser Support and Security

Service workers require HTTPS because they deal with potentially sensitive data and powerful APIs. This ensures that any data intercepted by the service worker is encrypted, providing a secure user experience.

Most modern browsers support service workers, but it's crucial to check compatibility and handle cases where the service worker might not be supported.

```
if ('serviceWorker' in navigator) {
  navigator.serviceWorker.register('/service-worker.js')
    .then(registration => {
      console.log('Service Worker registered with scope:', registration.scope);
    })
    .catch(error => {
      console.log('Service Worker registration failed:', error);
    });
}
```

Use Cases and Benefits

Service workers bring numerous benefits to your Vue.js PWA:

- **Improved Speed and Performance**: By caching key assets, service workers can drastically reduce load times.
- **Offline Availability**: Users can access your app even when they are offline.
- **Push Notifications**: Engage and re-engage users with timely notifications.
- **Network Resilience**: Handle flaky networks gracefully, ensuring a smooth user experience.

Understanding and integrating service workers into your Vue.js Progressive Web App is essential for delivering a robust, offline-capable, and performing application. In the next sections, we will delve deeper into registering a service worker, various caching strategies, and how to update and debug service workers efficiently.

8.2 Registering a Service Worker

Registering a Service Worker is a crucial step in transforming your Vue.js application into a fully functional Progressive Web App (PWA). By doing so, you can enable features like offline functionality, caching, and background sync. In this subchapter, we'll walk through the process of registering a Service Worker in a Vue.js application, ensuring that your app is ready to take advantage of the powerful capabilities that Service Workers offer.

Setting Up the Service Worker File

Before we can register a Service Worker, we need to create a Service Worker file. This file contains the JavaScript code that defines the behavior of your Service Worker. Typically, this file is placed in the public directory of your Vue.js project so that it is accessible from the root URL.

Create a file named service-worker.js in the public directory of your project:

```
// public/service-worker.js

self.addEventListener('install', event => {
  console.log('Service Worker installing.');
  // Perform install steps
});

self.addEventListener('activate', event => {
  console.log('Service Worker activating.');
  // Perform activate steps
});

self.addEventListener('fetch', event => {
  console.log('Fetching:', event.request.url);
  // Respond to requests
});
```

This file contains the basic lifecycle events: `install`, `activate`, and `fetch`. We will be expanding on these in later sections, but this is a good start.

Registering the Service Worker in Your Vue.js App

To register the Service Worker, we must include the registration code in our Vue.js application's entry point. This is typically the `main.js` file.

Open `src/main.js` and add the following code:

```js
// src/main.js

import { createApp } from 'vue';
import App from './App.vue';

createApp(App).mount('#app');

// Check if service workers are supported
if ('serviceWorker' in navigator) {
  window.addEventListener('load', () => {
    navigator.serviceWorker.register('/service-worker.js')
      .then(registration => {
        console.log('Service Worker registered with scope:', registration.scope);
      })
      .catch(error => {
        console.log('Service Worker registration failed:', error);
      });
  });
}
```

This script checks if the browser supports Service Workers and then waits for the `load` event before attempting to register the Service Worker. If the registration is successful, a confirmation is logged to the console along with the scope of the Service Worker. If there is an error during the registration process, it is caught and logged.

Verifying Service Worker Registration

After adding the registration code, start your Vue.js development server:

```
npm run serve
```

Open your application in a web browser and open the browser's Developer Tools (usually accessible by right-clicking the page and selecting "Inspect" or pressing Ctrl+Shift+I or Cmd+Opt+I). Navigate to the "Application" panel (in Chrome) or a similar tab in other browsers.

In the "Service Workers" section, you should see your Service Worker listed. It should show its status as "Activated" if everything is functioning correctly. You should also see the console logs from the install, activate, and fetch events if you have requests going through the Service Worker.

Handling Registration Failures

It's essential to handle possible failures when registering a Service Worker so that your application can gracefully degrade if something goes wrong. While the above example already includes basic error logging, you may want to provide more robust error handling depending on your application's requirements.

For example, you could notify users if the Service Worker registration fails:

```
navigator.serviceWorker.register('/service-worker.js')
  .then(registration => {
    console.log('Service Worker registered with scope:', registration.scope);
  })
  .catch(error => {
    console.log('Service Worker registration failed:', error);
    alert('Service Worker registration failed. Please try again later.');
  });
```

By incorporating user-friendly error messages, you ensure that your users are kept informed and can understand when something is not working as expected.

Conclusion

Registering a Service Worker is a straightforward yet critical step in building a PWA with Vue.js. By correctly setting up and registering your Service Worker, your application can start leveraging advanced features like offline support, better performance through caching, and background sync. This foundation will be expanded upon in the next sections, where we'll dive deeper into caching strategies and manage updates and debugging for your Service Worker.

8.3 Caching Strategies

Caching strategies are an essential part of optimizing the performance and reliability of Progressive Web Apps (PWAs). With the help of service workers, you can intercept network requests and define caching strategies that dictate how responses are stored and retrieved. In this subchapter, we will explore different caching strategies and provide examples of how to implement them using Vue.js.

Cache First Strategy

The **Cache First** strategy is a common approach where the service worker attempts to serve the content from the cache before making a network request. If the resource is found in the cache, it is served immediately; otherwise, a network request is made, and the response is saved in the cache for future use.

Example

```
self.addEventListener('fetch', event => {
  event.respondWith(
    caches.match(event.request).then(cacheResponse => {
      // Return the cache if it exists
      if (cacheResponse) {
        return cacheResponse;
      }

      // Otherwise, fetch from the network
      return fetch(event.request).then(networkResponse => {
        // Save the response to the cache for future use
        return caches.open('dynamic-cache').then(cache => {
          cache.put(event.request, networkResponse.clone())
;
          return networkResponse;
        });
      });
    })
  );
});
```

In this example, the service worker first checks the cache for the requested resource. If the resource is not found, it fetches it from the network and stores it in the cache.

Network First Strategy

The **Network First** strategy prioritizes fetching the latest content from the network. If the network request fails (e.g., due to being offline), the service worker serves the content from the cache.

Example

```
self.addEventListener('fetch', event => {
  event.respondWith(
    fetch(event.request).then(networkResponse => {
      // Save the response to the cache for future use
      return caches.open('dynamic-cache').then(cache => {
        cache.put(event.request, networkResponse.clone());
        return networkResponse;
      });
    }).catch(() => {
      // If network fetch fails, return the cached response
      return caches.match(event.request);
    })
  );
});
```

This strategy ensures that users always get the most up-to-date content when they are online, while still providing a fallback to cached content if they are offline.

Cache Only Strategy

The **Cache Only** strategy serves content solely from the cache, bypassing the network entirely. This strategy is useful for static assets that do not change often.

Example

```
self.addEventListener('fetch', event => {
  event.respondWith(
    caches.match(event.request)
  );
});
```

This approach is extremely fast but requires that all necessary assets are pre-cached.

Network Only Strategy

The **Network Only** strategy fetches all resources from the network, without caching them. This may be useful for API endpoints where cached data would be considered stale.

Example

```
self.addEventListener('fetch', event => {
  event.respondWith(fetch(event.request));
});
```

This strategy does not leverage the benefits of caching but ensures that the data is always current.

Stale-While-Revalidate Strategy

The **Stale-While-Revalidate** strategy serves content from the cache while simultaneously updating the cache with the latest response from the network. This provides a good balance between performance and freshness.

Example

```
self.addEventListener('fetch', event => {
  event.respondWith(
    caches.match(event.request).then(cacheResponse => {
      const fetchPromise = fetch(event.request).then(networkResponse => {
        caches.open('dynamic-cache').then(cache => {
          cache.put(event.request, networkResponse.clone())
;
        });
        return networkResponse;
      });
      return cacheResponse || fetchPromise;
    })
  );
});
```

In this strategy, the service worker serves the cached response immediately and updates the cache with the response from the network when it becomes available.

Utilizing Vue.js

When integrating these caching strategies into a Vue.js application, consider where and how the service worker script is registered and controlled. This typically occurs in the `main.js` file or a dedicated service worker registration file.

Example in a Vue.js App

```
// src/registerServiceWorker.js

if ('serviceWorker' in navigator) {
  navigator.serviceWorker.register('/service-worker.js').then(registration => {
      console.log('Service Worker registered with scope:', registration.scope);
  }).catch(error => {
      console.error('Service Worker registration failed:', error);
  });
}
```

By implementing these caching strategies, you can significantly enhance the performance and reliability of your Vue.js-based PWA, providing a seamless user experience even in challenging network conditions.

8.4 Updating and Debugging Service Workers

Service Worker Lifecycle

Service workers have a distinct lifecycle that includes installation, activation, and control. Fully understanding this lifecycle is vital for both updating and debugging service workers.

Updating a Service Worker

When you want to update a service worker, it's not sufficient to just upload a new version to your server. The browser will only re-download the service worker script if it has changed since the last installation.

Versioning Your Service Worker

A simple way to make sure your service worker updates correctly is to modify its script. You could even include a version number as a comment for clarity.

```
// Version 1.0.1
self.addEventListener('install', event => {
  console.log('Service Worker installing.');
  // Perform install steps
});
```

Forcing an Update

You can programmatically check for and force an update of the service worker. Use the `update` method provided by the `ServiceWorkerRegistration` interface.

```
navigator.serviceWorker.getRegistration().then(registration
=> {
  if (registration) {
    registration.update();
  }
});
```

Handling Service Worker Updates

When a new service worker is found, it will go through the install event, but it won't take control until the old service worker is finished. You can control this behavior by using the `skipWaiting` method within the install event.

```
self.addEventListener('install', event => {
  self.skipWaiting();
  console.log('Service Worker installed with skipWaiting.')
;
});
```

However, `skipWaiting` should be used cautiously, as it could interfere with any ongoing tasks that the old service worker is managing.

Activating the Updated Service Worker

Once the service worker has been installed, the next step is activation. During activation, you can clear out old caches and prepare for the service worker to take control.

```
self.addEventListener('activate', event => {
  event.waitUntil(
    caches.keys().then(cacheNames => {
      return Promise.all(
        cacheNames.map(cache => {
          if (cache !== newCacheName) {
            return caches.delete(cache);
          }
        })
      );
    })
  );
  console.log('Service Worker activated.');
});
```

Debugging Service Workers

Debugging service workers is a bit different from debugging regular JavaScript, given the unique constraints and lifecycle.

Using the Browser DevTools

Modern browsers provide excellent tools for debugging service workers. Here's how you can make use of them effectively:

70. **Open DevTools**: In Chrome, you can press `Ctrl + Shift + I` (Windows) or `Cmd + Option + I` (Mac) to open the Developer Tools.
71. **Go to Application Panel**: Navigate to the 'Application' panel.
72. **Service Workers Section**: Here you will see your registered service workers. You can inspect, update, and even unregister them.

Logging and Error Handling

Effective logging is crucial for debugging service workers. The `console` API works within service workers, allowing you to log messages to the browser console.

```
self.addEventListener('fetch', event => {
  console.log('Fetching:', event.request.url);

  event.respondWith(
    caches.match(event.request).then(response => {
      if (response) {
        console.log('Found in cache:', response);
        return response;
      }
      console.log('Network request for:', event.request.url
);
      return fetch(event.request);
    }).catch(error => {
      console.error('Fetch failed:', error);
      throw error;
    })
  );
});
```

Using Breakpoints

You can set breakpoints in your service worker script using the 'Sources' panel in DevTools. This can be incredibly useful to pause execution and inspect the current state.

Handling Errors Gracefully

It's important to handle errors gracefully within your service worker to ensure a good user experience.

```
self.addEventListener('fetch', event => {
  event.respondWith(
    fetch(event.request)
      .then(response => {
        if (!response || response.status !== 200 || response.type !== 'basic') {
          throw new Error('Network response was not ok');
        }
        return response;
      })
      .catch(error => {
        console.error('Fetching failed:', error);
        // Fallback to a default response or cached response
        return new Response('Fallback content', { status: 200 });
      })
  );
});
```

Inspecting Cache Storage

You can inspect the contents of your cache storage using the 'Application' panel in DevTools. This is useful for debugging what assets are being cached.

73. **Open DevTools** and navigate to the 'Application' panel.
74. **Expand Cache Storage**: Here you will see all caches.
75. **Inspect Each Cache**: Look inside each cache to see the stored assets.

By carefully managing updates and utilizing debugging tools, you can maintain an efficient, resilient, and user-friendly service worker in your Vue.js Progressive Web App.

9. Handling Offline Capabilities

9.1 Overview of Offline Capabilities

Progressive Web Apps (PWAs) are designed to provide a resilient user experience, even when network connectivity is unreliable or completely unavailable. Offline capabilities are a cornerstone of PWAs, enabling apps to function smoothly regardless of network conditions. This subchapter provides an overview of various strategies and tools used to handle offline scenarios in PWAs built with Vue.js.

The Importance of Offline Capabilities

The primary reason for implementing offline capabilities is to enhance user experience. Users expect applications to be accessible and functional whenever they need them, irrespective of their network status. Offline capabilities also contribute to reducing server load, improving performance, and increasing user retention.

Key Principles of Offline-First Design

76. **Cache-First Strategy**: Serve files from the cache whenever available, and fallback to the network if not. This ensures that users can access the application even without an internet connection.

77. **Graceful Degradation**: Ensure that essential app features remain functional offline, while non-essential features may degrade gracefully.

78. **Data Synchronization**: Implement mechanisms to synchronize data between the client and server once the connection is restored.

Service Workers

Service workers play a crucial role in enabling offline capabilities. They are scripts that run in the background, separate from the web page, intercepting network requests and serving cached responses.

To register a service worker in a Vue.js application, add the following code in your `main.js` file:

```
if ('serviceWorker' in navigator) {
  navigator.serviceWorker.register('/service-worker.js')
    .then((registration) => {
      console.log('Service Worker registered with scope:', registration.scope);
    })
    .catch((error) => {
      console.log('Service Worker registration failed:', error);
    });
}
```

Caching Assets

Caching is one of the primary methods to ensure an app works offline. Service workers can cache essential assets like JavaScript, CSS, and images. Here's a simple example of a service worker that caches application assets:

```
const CACHE_NAME = 'my-pwa-cache-v1';
const urlsToCache = [
  '/',
  '/index.html',
  '/styles.css',
  '/app.js',
  '/offline.html' // Fallback page for offline mode
];

self.addEventListener('install', (event) => {
  event.waitUntil(
    caches.open(CACHE_NAME)
      .then((cache) => {
        return cache.addAll(urlsToCache);
      })
  );
});

self.addEventListener('fetch', (event) => {
  event.respondWith(
    caches.match(event.request)
      .then((response) => {
        return response || fetch(event.request);
      })
  );
});
```

IndexDB for Client-Side Storage

IndexDB can be utilized for storing large datasets that need to be accessed offline. Unlike localStorage, IndexDB is designed for high-performance reads and writes, making it ideal for complex applications.

Here's how you can store and retrieve data in IndexDB:

```js
const dbRequest = indexedDB.open('myDatabase', 1);

dbRequest.onupgradeneeded = (event) => {
  const db = event.target.result;
  db.createObjectStore('myStore', { keyPath: 'id' });
};

dbRequest.onsuccess = (event) => {
  const db = event.target.result;

  // Adding data
  const transaction = db.transaction(['myStore'], 'readwrite');
  const store = transaction.objectStore('myStore');
  store.add({ id: 1, name: 'Vue.js' });

  // Retrieving data
  const request = store.get(1);
  request.onsuccess = () => {
    console.log('Data:', request.result);
  };
};
```

Fallback Pages

Creating fallback pages is another essential aspect. For instance, displaying a custom offline page when the user has no internet connection.

```html
<!-- offline.html -->
<!DOCTYPE html>
<html>
<head>
  <title>Offline</title>
  <style>
    body { text-align: center; padding: 50px; font-family: Arial, sans-serif; }
  </style>
</head>
<body>
  <h1>You are offline.</h1>
  <p>Please check your internet connection.</p>
</body>
</html>
```

By pre-caching these pages and delivering them when network requests fail, you provide a better user experience.

Conclusion

With offline capabilities, a Vue.js-based PWA becomes more reliable and user-friendly. By leveraging service workers, caching strategies, IndexDB, and fallback mechanisms, developers can create applications that gracefully handle network disruptions. The subsequent sections will dive deeper into specific techniques and code implementations to manage offline capabilities effectively.

9.2 Service Workers and Caching Strategies

Service workers form the backbone of offline capabilities for Progressive Web Apps (PWAs). They operate in the background, intercepting network requests and serving cached resources when a network is unavailable, thus enhancing the user experience during offline scenarios. This subchapter focuses on how to effectively use service workers and implement various caching strategies in your Vue.js PWA.

Introduction to Service Workers

Service workers are background scripts that operate independently from the web page. This independence allows them to handle network requests, manage caching, and deliver push notifications.

To register a service worker in your Vue.js project, you can add the following code to your `main.js` file:

```
if ('serviceWorker' in navigator) {
  window.addEventListener('load', () => {
    navigator.serviceWorker.register('/service-worker.js')
      .then(registration => {
        console.log('ServiceWorker registration successful with scope: ', registration.scope);
      })
      .catch(error => {
        console.log('ServiceWorker registration failed: ', error);
      });
  });
}
```

In this example, the service worker script is located at `/service-worker.js`.

Implementing a Basic Service Worker

A basic service worker script might look like the following:

```js
const CACHE_NAME = 'my-app-cache-v1';
const urlsToCache = [
  '/',
  '/index.html',
  '/styles.css',
  '/script.js'
];

self.addEventListener('install', event => {
  event.waitUntil(
    caches.open(CACHE_NAME)
      .then(cache => {
        console.log('Opened cache');
        return cache.addAll(urlsToCache);
      })
  );
});

self.addEventListener('fetch', event => {
  event.respondWith(
    caches.match(event.request)
      .then(response => {
        return response || fetch(event.request);
      })
  );
});
```

In this script: - The `install` event is used to open the specified cache and add the specified URLs to it. - The `fetch` event intercepts network requests and responds with cached responses if they are available, otherwise it fetches the request from the network.

Caching Strategies

Caching strategies define how and when resources should be cached and served. The main strategies include:

Cache First

The Cache First strategy serves resources from the cache if available, falling back to the network if the resource is not in the cache.

```
self.addEventListener('fetch', event => {
  event.respondWith(
    caches.match(event.request)
      .then(response => {
        if (response) {
          return response;
        }
        return fetch(event.request);
      })
  );
});
```

This strategy is beneficial for assets that rarely change, such as static images or site logos.

Network First

The Network First strategy tries to fetch resources from the network first and falls back to the cache if the network is unavailable.

```
self.addEventListener('fetch', event => {
  event.respondWith(
    fetch(event.request)
      .then(response => {
        if (!response || response.status !== 200) {
          throw new Error('Network response was not ok');
        }
        let responseClone = response.clone();
        caches.open(CACHE_NAME)
          .then(cache => {
            cache.put(event.request, responseClone);
          });
        return response;
      })
      .catch(() => caches.match(event.request))
  );
});
```

This strategy is ideal for dynamic content, like an API response that requires up-to-date information.

Stale-While-Revalidate

The Stale-While-Revalidate strategy serves cached content immediately while fetching updated content from the network. The newly fetched content is then cached for future use.

```
self.addEventListener('fetch', event => {
  event.respondWith(
    caches.match(event.request).then(response => {
      let fetchPromise = fetch(event.request).then(networkR
esponse => {
        caches.open(CACHE_NAME).then(cache => {
          cache.put(event.request, networkResponse.clone())
;
        });
        return networkResponse;
      });
      return response || fetchPromise;
    })
  );
});
```

This approach offers a balance between performance and fresh data, making it particularly useful for fast responses with background updates.

Conclusion

Understanding and implementing the appropriate caching strategies is crucial for delivering a seamless offline experience in your Vue.js PWA. By leveraging service workers effectively, you can ensure that users have access to your app's critical resources even when they're offline, thus enhancing the overall reliability and usability of your PWA.

9.3 Handling Data Synchronization

Handling data synchronization in a Progressive Web App (PWA) is crucial for ensuring a seamless user experience, especially when the app needs to operate both online and offline. Synchronization involves keeping data consistent between the client (browser) and the server, ensuring that any changes made while offline are correctly updated when the app goes online again.

Challenges of Data Synchronization

Synchronizing data in web applications comes with its set of challenges, including:

- **Conflict Resolution:** Ensuring that any conflicting updates made by different users at different times are managed correctly.
- **Network Variability:** Handling the transitions between offline and online states without data loss.
- **Data Integrity:** Maintaining the consistency and integrity of the data across the client and server.

Strategies for Data Synchronization

There are different strategies you can employ to handle data synchronization in Vue.js PWAs:

- **Background Sync:** Utilize the Background Sync API to defer data synchronization until the user has a stable internet connection.
- **IndexedDB:** Store data locally using IndexedDB when offline and sync it with the server once connectivity is restored.

- **Conflict Resolution Logic:** Implement logic to manage conflicts, such as merging changes or prompting users to resolve conflicts.

Implementing Background Sync

Background Sync is an excellent way to handle deferred operations, like sending data to the server, when the internet connection is restored. Here's a basic example:

79. **Register Background Sync in Service Worker:**

```javascript
self.addEventListener('sync', function(event) {
  if (event.tag === 'sync-data') {
    event.waitUntil(syncData());
  }
});

function syncData() {
  return getDataFromIndexedDB().then(data => {
    return fetch('https://yourapi.com/sync', {
      method: 'POST',
      body: JSON.stringify(data),
      headers: {
        'Content-Type': 'application/json'
      }
    });
  });
}
```

2. **Request Sync from the Client:**

```javascript
navigator.serviceWorker.ready.then(function(registration) {
  return registration.sync.register('sync-data');
});
```

Using IndexedDB for Local Storage

IndexedDB is a low-level API for storing significant amounts of structured data, including files and blobs. Here's how you can use IndexedDB to store data offline:

80. **Open or Create a Database:**

```
let db;
const request = indexedDB.open('myDatabase', 1);

request.onsuccess = function(event) {
  db = event.target.result;
};

request.onupgradeneeded = function(event) {
  db = event.target.result;
  const store = db.createObjectStore('posts', { keyPath: 'id' });
};
```

3. **Store Data Offline:**

```
function savePost(post) {
  const transaction = db.transaction(['posts'], 'readwrite');
  const store = transaction.objectStore('posts');
  store.put(post);
}
```

Synchronizing Data Upon Connectivity Restoration

When the internet connection is restored, you can synchronize the locally stored data with the server:

81. **Detect Online Status:**

```
window.addEventListener('online', () => {
  syncLocalDataWithServer();
});
```

4. **Synchronize Data:**

```
function syncLocalDataWithServer() {
  const transaction = db.transaction(['posts'], 'readonly')
;
  const store = transaction.objectStore('posts');
  const request = store.getAll();

  request.onsuccess = function() {
    const posts = request.result;
    posts.forEach(post => {
      fetch('https://yourapi.com/posts', {
        method: 'POST',
        body: JSON.stringify(post),
        headers: {
          'Content-Type': 'application/json'
        }
      }).then(() => {
        // Optionally delete from IndexedDB after successful sync
      });
    });
  };
}
```

Handling Conflicts

When both the client and server update the same data, conflicts can occur. Here's a basic conflict-handling strategy:

82. **Version Control:** Use version numbers to determine which data is more recent.

```
function resolveConflict(localData, serverData) {
  if (localData.version > serverData.version) {
    return localData;
  } else {
    return serverData;
  }
}
```

5. **Merge Changes:** Merge changes from both versions where possible, which might involve more complex logic specific to your application's needs.

Conclusion

Handling data synchronization efficiently is vital for creating responsive and robust Progressive Web Apps with Vue.js. Leveraging Background Sync, IndexedDB, and well-thought-out conflict resolution strategies ensures that your app provides a seamless user experience, whether online or offline. By understanding these essential techniques, you're well on your way to mastering offline capabilities in PWAs.

9.4 Managing Offline Notifications

When building a Progressive Web App (PWA) with Vue.js, managing offline notifications is crucial to enhancing user experience. Offline notifications help inform users about their connectivity status, actions taken, or needed attention when they are not connected to the internet. This subchapter will cover strategies and code examples for implementing offline notifications using Vue.js.

Importance of Offline Notifications

Offline notifications play a key role in improving the user experience in the following ways: 1. **User Awareness**: They inform users when they are offline, helping them understand why certain functionalities might not be available. 2. **Data Synchronization**: Users are notified when data is being stored locally and will be synchronized once they regain connectivity. 3. **Interaction Feedback**: Providing feedback on user actions when offline ensures they are aware that their actions have been queued for later processing.

Creating a Notification System

To manage offline notifications in a Vue.js PWA, we will create a notification system that listens for changes in connectivity status and displays appropriate messages to the user.

Notification Component

First, create a Notification component that will be responsible for displaying messages to the user.

Notification.vue

```
<template>
  <div v-if="show" class="notification" :class="type">
    <p>{{ message }}</p>
    <button @click="dismiss()">Dismiss</button>
  </div>
</template>

<script>
export default {
  props: {
    message: String,
    type: {
      type: String,
      default: 'info'
    }
  },
  data() {
    return {
      show: true
    };
  },
  methods: {
    dismiss() {
      this.show = false;
    }
  }
};
</script>

<style>
.notification {
  position: fixed;
  bottom: 20px;
  right: 20px;
  padding: 10px;
  border-radius: 5px;
  background-color: #444;
  color: #fff;
}
.notification.info {
  background-color: #007BFF;
}
.notification.error {
  background-color: #DC3545;
}
.notification.success {
  background-color: #28A745;
```

```
}
</style>
```

Managing Connectivity Status

Next, we need to monitor the user's connectivity status using the `navigator.onLine` property and the `online` and `offline` events. We can create a mixin to handle these events and manage the display of notifications accordingly.

connectivityMixin.js

```js
import Notification from '@/components/Notification.vue';

export default {
  components: {
    Notification
  },
  data() {
    return {
      isOnline: navigator.onLine,
      notifications: []
    };
  },
  created() {
    window.addEventListener('online', this.updateOnlineStatus);
    window.addEventListener('offline', this.updateOnlineStatus);
  },
  beforeDestroy() {
    window.removeEventListener('online', this.updateOnlineStatus);
    window.removeEventListener('offline', this.updateOnlineStatus);
  },
  methods: {
    updateOnlineStatus() {
      this.isOnline = navigator.onLine;
      if (this.isOnline) {
        this.addNotification('You are back online!', 'success');
      } else {
        this.addNotification('You are offline. Some functionalities may be limited.', 'error');
      }
    },
    addNotification(message, type) {
      this.notifications.push({ message, type });
    }
  }
};
```

Integrating Mixin with the App

To integrate the connectivity mixin with your Vue.js app, import the mixin into your main application component or any relevant components.

App.vue

```
<template>
  <div id="app">
    <!-- other app content -->
    <notification v-for="(notification, index) in notifications"
                  :key="index"
                  :message="notification.message"
                  :type="notification.type" />
  </div>
</template>

<script>
import connectivityMixin from '@/mixins/connectivityMixin.js';

export default {
  mixins: [connectivityMixin],
  // other component options
};
</script>
```

Enhancing Notification System

To further enhance your notification system, consider integrating it with a Vuex store for centralized state management. This allows easier tracking and control of notifications across your app.

Store Setup

83. **Install Vuex if it's not already installed**: bash   npm install vuex

84. **Create Vuex Store Module for Notifications**:

store/notifications.js

```
export default {
  state: {
    notifications: []
  },
  mutations: {
    ADD_NOTIFICATION(state, { message, type }) {
      state.notifications.push({ message, type });
    },
    REMOVE_NOTIFICATION(state, index) {
      state.notifications.splice(index, 1);
    }
  },
  actions: {
    addNotification({ commit }, { message, type }) {
      commit('ADD_NOTIFICATION', { message, type });
    },
    removeNotification({ commit }, index) {
      commit('REMOVE_NOTIFICATION', index);
    }
  }
};
```

3. **Integrate Notification Module into Vuex Store**:

store/index.js

```
import Vue from 'vue';
import Vuex from 'vuex';
import notifications from './notifications.js';

Vue.use(Vuex);

export default new Vuex.Store({
  modules: {
    notifications
  }
});
```

4. **Update Mixin to Use Vuex Store**:

connectivityMixin.js

```
export default {
  computed: {
    notifications() {
      return this.$store.state.notifications.notifications;
    }
  },
  created() {
    window.addEventListener('online', this.updateOnlineStat
us);
    window.addEventListener('offline', this.updateOnlineSta
tus);
  },
  beforeDestroy() {
    window.removeEventListener('online', this.updateOnlineS
tatus);
    window.removeEventListener('offline', this.updateOnline
Status);
  },
  methods: {
    updateOnlineStatus() {
      if (navigator.onLine) {
        this.$store.dispatch('addNotification', { message:
'You are back online!', type: 'success' });
      } else {
        this.$store.dispatch('addNotification', { message:
'You are offline. Some functionalities may be limited.', ty
pe: 'error' });
      }
    }
  }
};
```

Conclusion

Managing offline notifications in your Vue.js PWA ensures that users are well-informed about their connectivity status and any resulting actions. By creating a robust notification system and leveraging Vuex for state management, you can significantly improve the user experience in offline scenarios.

10. Performance Optimization Techniques

10.1 Code Splitting and Lazy Loading

As web applications grow in complexity and size, managing the load times and performance becomes crucial. One effective technique to optimize performance in Vue.js-driven Progressive Web Apps (PWAs) is through code splitting and lazy loading. This subchapter delves into how you can implement these strategies to create faster, more efficient web applications.

What is Code Splitting?

Code splitting is a frontend optimization technique that breaks down your application into smaller chunks, which are only loaded when needed. Instead of delivering a single, large JavaScript file to users, code splitting ensures that your application loads only the necessary sections dynamically. This leads to faster initial load times and improved performance.

Implementing Code Splitting in Vue.js

Vue.js leverages Webpack under the hood, which makes code splitting straightforward. You can use dynamic `import()` statements within your Vue components to split your code at a route level or component level.

Dynamic `import()` with Vue Router

Vue Router supports lazy loading out of the box. Here's how you can set up code splitting with Vue Router:

```js
// router/index.js
import Vue from 'vue';
import Router from 'vue-router';

Vue.use(Router);

const routes = [
  {
    path: '/home',
    name: 'Home',
    component: () => import('@/views/Home.vue')
  },
  {
    path: '/about',
    name: 'About',
    component: () => import('@/views/About.vue')
  }
];

export default new Router({
  mode: 'history', // or 'hash'
  routes
});
```

In this example, the Home.vue and About.vue components are dynamically imported. They will only be loaded when their respective routes are visited, reducing the initial bundle size.

Lazy Loading Components

You can also apply code splitting at the component level. This is particularly useful for components that are not tied to a specific route but may be conditionally rendered within a template.

```
// ParentComponent.vue
<template>
  <div>
    <button @click="showChildComponent = true">Load Component</button>
    <Suspense>
      <template #default>
        <ChildComponent v-if="showChildComponent" />
      </template>
      <template #fallback>
        <div>Loading...</div>
      </template>
    </Suspense>
  </div>
</template>

<script>
import { defineAsyncComponent } from 'vue';

export default {
  components: {
    ChildComponent: defineAsyncComponent(() => import('@/components/ChildComponent.vue'))
  },
  data() {
    return {
      showChildComponent: false
    };
  }
};
</script>
```

In this example, `ChildComponent` is lazily loaded when the button is clicked. The `Suspense` tag provides a way to show a loading indicator while the component is being fetched.

Benefits of Lazy Loading

Lazy loading is the practice of delaying the loading of resources until they are actually needed. When combined with code splitting, it can significantly reduce the initial load time and memory consumption of your application.

Example of Lazy Loading in Practice

```vue
// App.vue
<template>
  <div id="app">
    <HeaderComponent />
    <router-view />
    <FooterComponent />
  </div>
</template>

<script>
import HeaderComponent from '@/components/HeaderComponent.vue';
import FooterComponent from '@/components/FooterComponent.vue';

export default {
  components: {
    HeaderComponent,
    FooterComponent
  }
};
</script>
```

In this scenario, the `HeaderComponent` and `FooterComponent` are loaded eagerly with the application, while the components within the `router-view` are lazy loaded based on the route visited.

Using Webpack for Code Splitting

Webpack provides several methods for code splitting, including:

- **Dynamic Imports:** As demonstrated with `import()`, which splits code at import time.
- **Magic Comments:** You can use Webpack's magic comments for chunk naming.

```
// router/index.js
const routes = [
  {
    path: '/contact',
    name: 'Contact',
    component: () => import(/* webpackChunkName: "contact" */ '@/views/Contact.vue')
  }
];
```

Here, the file `Contact.vue` will be bundled into a separate chunk named "contact", which makes debugging easier.

Conclusion

Code splitting and lazy loading are essential techniques for optimizing the performance of Vue.js-powered PWAs. By implementing these strategies, you reduce the initial load time and ensure that your application remains fast and responsive. This not only improves user experience but also helps in maintaining a scalable codebase.

10.2 Efficient State Management

Efficient state management is crucial for optimizing the performance of your Progressive Web App (PWA) built with Vue.js. When managed effectively, state management can significantly improve your app's responsiveness and user experience. Vuex—the state management library for Vue.js—plays a pivotal role in maintaining a seamless flow of data across the application. This subchapter explores best practices for efficient state management using Vuex.

Avoiding State Bloat

State bloat occurs when your Vuex store holds more data than necessary, leading to increased memory consumption and slower state mutations or access. To prevent state bloat:

85. **Store Only Necessary Data:** Only keep data in Vuex that needs to be accessible across multiple components. Localize state to components when possible.
86. **Use Modular Stores:** Divide your store into modules, each responsible for a distinct part of the state. This keeps your store organized and manageable.

```js
const moduleA = {
    state: () => ({
        // State specific to moduleA
    }),
    mutations: {
        // Mutations for moduleA
    },
    actions: {
        // Actions for moduleA
    },
    getters: {
        // Getters for moduleA
    }
};

const moduleB = {
    state: () => ({
        // State specific to moduleB
    }),
    mutations: {
        // Mutations for moduleB
    },
    actions: {
        // Actions for moduleB
    },
    getters: {
        // Getters for moduleB
    }
};

const store = new Vuex.Store({
    modules: {
        a: moduleA,
        b: moduleB
    }
});
```

Leveraging Getters for Computed State

Getters in Vuex resemble computed properties in Vue components—they allow you to compute derived state based on the store's state. Using getters can help in reducing the need to store redundant data.

```
const store = new Vuex.Store({
    state: {
        items: [
            {id: 1, value: 10},
            {id: 2, value: 20}
        ],
        filterCriteria: 15
    },
    getters: {
        filteredItems: state => {
            return state.items.filter(item => item.value >=
state.filterCriteria);
        }
    }
});
```

Optimizing Mutations and Actions

Mutations and actions are the core aspects of Vuex for updating the state. Optimizing how you write these can lead to performance improvements.

87. **Batch Mutations:** Group related state changes into a single mutation to reduce the number of re-renders.

```
// Bad: Multiple mutations
mutations: {
    incrementValue1(state) {
        state.value1 += 1;
    },
    incrementValue2(state) {
        state.value2 += 1;
    }
}

// Good: Batched mutation
mutations: {
    incrementValues(state) {
        state.value1 += 1;
        state.value2 += 1;
    }
}
```

2. **Debounce Expensive Actions:** Use debouncing for actions that trigger expensive operations like network requests or complex calculations.

```
let timeout;
const actions = {
    fetchData({ commit }, payload) {
        clearTimeout(timeout);
        timeout = setTimeout(() => {
            // Fetch data from API
            fetch(`https://api.example.com/data?id=${payload}`)
                .then(response => response.json())
                .then(data => {
                    commit('setData', data);
                });
        }, 300); // Debouncing by 300ms
    }
};
```

Persisting State with Local Storage

Persisting Vuex state using local storage can enhance performance by reducing the need to repeatedly fetch the same data from remote servers.

```
import createPersistedState from 'vuex-persistedstate';

const store = new Vuex.Store({
    state: {
        // Your state properties
    },
    mutations: {
        // Your mutations
    },
    actions: {
        // Your actions
    },
    plugins: [createPersistedState()]
});
```

Avoiding Unnecessary State Updates

Ensure that state is not updated unnecessarily to avoid excessive re-renders and performance bottlenecks.

88. **Conditional Mutations:** Check if the new state differs from the current state before committing a mutation.

```
mutations: {
    setName(state, newName) {
        if (state.name !== newName) {
            state.name = newName;
        }
    }
}
```

Using Immutable Data Structures

Immutable data structures can be beneficial in ensuring that state changes are predictable and efficient. Libraries like Immutable.js can be integrated with Vuex to maintain immutable state.

```
import { Map } from 'immutable';

const state = {
    user: Map({
        name: 'John Doe',
        age: 30
    })
};

const mutations = {
    updateUser(state, newUser) {
        state.user = state.user.merge(newUser);
    }
};
```

By focusing on these best practices and techniques, you can achieve efficient state management in your Vue.js applications, ensuring optimal performance and a superior user experience.

10.3 Optimizing Network Performance

Optimizing network performance is critical for delivering a smooth and responsive experience in any web application, especially in Progressive Web Apps (PWAs). Network delays and inefficient data handling can lead to slow load times and a subpar user experience. In this subchapter, we will explore various techniques to optimize network performance in your Vue.js-based PWA.

Understanding Network Bottlenecks

Before diving into optimization techniques, it's essential to understand common network bottlenecks: - **Latency**: Time delay in data transfer. - **Throughput**: Amount of data transmitted over a connection in a given time. - **Payload Size**: Size of the data being transferred. - **Number of Requests**: Multiple HTTP requests can increase load times.

Reducing Payload Size

A large payload can drastically increase load times. Compressing your data can mitigate this issue.

JSON Compression

If you're dealing with JSON data, compress the payload using a suitable middleware on the server.

Example: Compress JSON response on Node.js server

```js
const express = require('express');
const compression = require('compression');
const app = express();

app.use(compression());

app.get('/data', (req, res) => {
    const largeData = {
        // Large JSON data
    };
    res.json(largeData);
});

app.listen(3000, () => console.log('Server running on port 3000'));
```

Minifying Static Assets

Ensure that your CSS, JavaScript, and HTML files are minified to reduce their size.

Example: Using Webpack for JS/CSS/HTML minification

```js
// webpack.config.js
const TerserPlugin = require('terser-webpack-plugin');
const MiniCssExtractPlugin = require('mini-css-extract-plugin');
const HtmlWebpackPlugin = require('html-webpack-plugin');

module.exports = {
    optimization: {
        minimize: true,
        minimizer: [new TerserPlugin()],
    },
    plugins: [
        new MiniCssExtractPlugin({
            filename: '[name].[contenthash].css',
        }),
        new HtmlWebpackPlugin({
            template: './src/index.html',
            minify: {
                collapseWhitespace: true,
                removeComments: true,
            },
        }),
    ],
};
```

Reducing the Number of Requests

Reduce the number of network requests by combining files and using techniques like HTTP/2 multiplexing or bundling assets.

Image Sprites

Combine multiple images into a single sprite to reduce HTTP requests.

Example: Using CSS to display image sprite sections

```css
.sprite {
    background: url('/images/sprite.png') no-repeat;
}

.sprite-icon1 {
    width: 32px;
    height: 32px;
    background-position: -10px -10px;
}

.sprite-icon2 {
    width: 32px;
    height: 32px;
    background-position: -50px -10px;
}
```

Implementing Lazy Loading for Images

Lazy loading images ensures that only the images in the viewport are loaded, significantly reducing the initial load time.

Example: Lazy loading with Vue.js

```
<template>
    <img v-lazy="image.url" alt="Description">
</template>

<script>
export default {
    data() {
        return {
            image: {
                url: 'https://example.com/large-image.jpg'
            }
        };
    }
};
</script>

<!-- Add vue-lazyload plugin -->
import Vue from 'vue';
import VueLazyload from 'vue-lazyload';

Vue.use(VueLazyload, {
    preLoad: 1.3,
    error: 'https://example.com/error.png',
    loading: 'https://example.com/loading.gif',
    attempt: 1,
});
```

Utilizing HTTP/2

HTTP/2 can significantly improve network performance by allowing multiple requests over a single connection and reducing latency.

Example: Enabling HTTP/2 in a Node.js Server

```js
const http2 = require('http2');
const fs = require('fs');

const server = http2.createSecureServer({
    key: fs.readFileSync('/path/to/privkey.pem'),
    cert: fs.readFileSync('/path/to/fullchain.pem')
});

server.on('stream', (stream, headers) => {
    stream.respond({
        'content-type': 'text/html; charset=utf-8',
        ':status': 200
    });
    stream.end('<h1>Hello HTTP/2!</h1>');
});

server.listen(8443, () => console.log('Server running on port 8443'));
```

Leveraging Service Workers

Service workers can cache resources effectively, reducing network requests and enabling offline capabilities.

Example: Caching with Service Workers

```
self.addEventListener('install', (event) => {
    event.waitUntil(
        caches.open('v1').then((cache) => {
            return cache.addAll([
                '/',
                '/index.html',
                '/styles.css',
                'https://example.com/some-external-resource
'
            ]);
        })
    );
});

self.addEventListener('fetch', (event) => {
    event.respondWith(
        caches.match(event.request).then((response) => {
            return response || fetch(event.request);
        })
    );
});
```

By implementing these network optimization techniques, you can ensure that your Vue.js-based Progressive Web App delivers a swift and efficient user experience. The methods outlined will help minimize load times, reduce latency, and handle data more efficiently, contributing to a robust and performant PWA.

10.4 Utilizing Browser Caching

Effective browser caching can significantly boost the performance of your Progressive Web App (PWA) built with Vue.js. By leveraging the browser's cache, you can reduce network latency, decrease the load on your servers, and improve the overall user experience. In this subchapter, we'll explore various strategies for utilizing browser caching, including setting proper cache headers, using Service Workers, and leveraging Vue.js primitives to enhance caching.

Browser Caching Basics

Browser caching allows you to store web resources (like HTML, CSS, JavaScript, and images) locally on a user's machine, which can then be reused for subsequent requests. This reduces the need to fetch resources from the server each time a user visits your app. The primary mechanisms to control browser caching are HTTP headers including Cache-Control, Expires, and ETag.

Setting Cache-Control Headers

The Cache-Control header defines directives for caching mechanisms in both requests and responses. You can use this header to specify how long and under what conditions resources should be stored in the cache.

Example of setting Cache-Control headers in your Vue.js application via an Express server:

```javascript
const express = require('express');
const path = require('path');
const app = express();

app.use(express.static('public', {
  maxAge: '1y',   // Cache for 1 year
  etag: false,    // Disable etags
  setHeaders: (res, path) => {
    if (path.endsWith('.html')) {
      res.setHeader('Cache-Control', 'public, max-age=0');
    }
  }
}));

app.listen(3000, () => {
  console.log('Server running on http://localhost:3000');
});
```

Using Expires Headers

The `Expires` header specifies an absolute date and time after which the resource is considered stale. Unlike `Cache-Control`, it works with older HTTP 1.0 clients.

Example:

```
Expires: Wed, 21 Oct 2023 07:28:00 GMT
```

Leveraging Service Workers

Service Workers provide more fine-grained control over caching and are fundamental to the operation of a PWA. By caching resources directly in the Service Worker, you can ensure that your application works offline and improves response times for repeat visits.

Service Worker `install` event example for caching:

```
self.addEventListener('install', event => {
  event.waitUntil(
    caches.open('v1').then(cache => {
      return cache.addAll([
        '/index.html',
        '/styles.css',
        '/script.js',
        '/logo.png'
      ]);
    })
  );
});

self.addEventListener('fetch', event => {
  event.respondWith(
    caches.match(event.request).then(response => {
      return response || fetch(event.request);
    })
  );
});
```

Implementing Vue.js Primitives for Caching

In addition to HTTP headers and Service Workers, Vue.js itself offers primitives that can be used to enhance caching. Using techniques like component caching and data caching can help make your Vue.js application even more performant.

Component Caching with `keep-alive`

Vue's `keep-alive` component can be used to cache components that are not actively being used but still should remain in memory.

Example:

```html
<template>
  <div id="app">
    <keep-alive>
      <router-view v-if="$route.meta.keepAlive" />
    </keep-alive>
    <router-view v-else />
  </div>
</template>

<script>
export default {
  name: 'App'
};
</script>
```

In your router configuration:

```js
const routes = [
  {
    path: '/home',
    component: Home,
    meta: { keepAlive: true }
  },
  {
    path: '/about',
    component: About
  }
];
```

Data Caching with Vuex

Caching API responses at the state management level can significantly reduce unnecessary network requests. Vuex can be configured to implement simple data caching strategies.

Example of a Vuex action with data caching:

```js
const store = new Vuex.Store({
  state: {
    items: [],
    LastFetched: null
  },
  actions: {
    async fetchItems({ commit, state }) {
      if (state.items.length > 0 && Date.now() - state.LastFetched < 60000) {
        return; // Use cached data if less than 1 minute old
      }

      const response = await fetch('https://your-api-url.com/items');
      const data = await response.json();
      commit('setItems', data);
      commit('setLastFetched', Date.now());
    }
  },
  mutations: {
    setItems(state, items) {
      state.items = items;
    },
    setLastFetched(state, timestamp) {
      state.LastFetched = timestamp;
    }
  }
});
```

In your component:

```js
export default {
  created() {
    this.$store.dispatch('fetchItems');
  },
  computed: {
    items() {
      return this.$store.state.items;
    }
  }
};
```

Summary

Utilizing browser caching effectively involves a multi-layered approach, incorporating HTTP headers, Service Workers, and Vue.js specific caching mechanisms. By understanding and implementing these strategies, you can significantly improve the performance of your Progressive Web App, reduce server load, and offer a smoother user experience.

11. Testing and Debugging Your PWA

11.1 Setting Up Your Testing Environment

Setting up a robust testing environment is essential for ensuring the reliability and functionality of your Progressive Web App (PWA). This subchapter will guide you through the process of setting up your testing environment for a Vue.js-based PWA. We'll cover the configuration of essential tools for unit testing and end-to-end (E2E) testing.

Prerequisites

Before we delve into the setup, ensure you have the following prerequisites:

- Node.js installed on your machine. You can download it from https://nodejs.org/
- A Vue.js project set up. Refer to Chapter 4, "Creating Your First Vue.js App," for guidance.

Installing Required Packages

First, let's install the necessary testing libraries. We will use Jest for unit testing and Cypress for end-to-end testing. Run the following commands to install these packages:

```
npm install --save-dev jest vue-jest babel-jest @vue/test-utils
npm install --save-dev cypress
```

Setting Up Jest for Unit Testing

Jest is a delightful JavaScript testing framework with a focus on simplicity. Follow these steps to set up Jest in your Vue.js project:

89. **Create a Jest Configuration File**

    Create a file named `jest.config.js` in the root of your project with the following content:

    ```
    module.exports = {
      moduleFileExtensions: ["js", "json", "vue"],
      transform: {
        "^.+\\.js$": "babel-jest",
        ".*\\.(vue)$": "vue-jest",
      },
      testMatch: ["**/tests/unit/**/*.spec.(js|jsx|ts|tsx)"],
      moduleNameMapper: {
        "^@/(.*)$": "<rootDir>/src/$1",
      },
    };
    ```

90. **Add Test Scripts to `package.json`**

    Add the following scripts to your `package.json` file under the `"scripts"` section:

    ```
    "scripts": {
      "test:unit": "jest"
    }
    ```

91. **Create a Sample Unit Test**

    Create a directory named `tests/unit` and a file named `example.spec.js` with the following content:

    ```
    import { shallowMount } from "@vue/test-utils";
    import ExampleComponent from "@/components/ExampleCom
    poncnt.vue";

    describe("ExampleComponent.vue", () => {
      it("renders props.msg when passed", () => {
        const msg = "new message";
        const wrapper = shallowMount(ExampleComponent, {
    ```

```
        propsData: { msg },
    });
        expect(wrapper.text()).toMatch(msg);
    });
});
```

Setting Up Cypress for End-to-End Testing

Cypress is a next-generation front-end testing tool built for the modern web. Follow these steps to integrate Cypress into your Vue.js project:

92. **Install Cypress**

    If you haven't already, run the following command to install Cypress:

    ```
    npm install --save-dev cypress
    ```

93. **Add Cypress Configuration File**

    Create a directory named `cypress` at the root of your project and add a file named `cypress.json` with the following content:

    ```
    {
      "baseUrl": "http://localhost:8080",
      "integrationFolder": "cypress/integration",
      "video": false
    }
    ```

94. **Add Test Scripts to `package.json`**

    Add the following scripts to your `package.json` file under the `"scripts"` section:

    ```
    "scripts": {
      "test:e2e": "cypress open"
    }
    ```

95. **Create a Sample End-to-End Test**

Create a directory named `cypress/integration` and a file named `example.spec.js` with the following content:

```
describe('My First Test', () => {
  it('Visits the app root url', () => {
    cy.visit('/');
    cy.contains('h1', 'Welcome to Your Vue.js App');
  });
});
```

96. **Running Cypress**

You can now run Cypress with the following command:

`npm run test:e2e`

This will open the Cypress Test Runner, where you can run your end-to-end tests.

Directory Structure

After setting up your testing environment, your Vue.js project directory structure should look something like this:

```
project-root/
├── cypress/
│   ├── integration/
│   │   └── example.spec.js
│   └── cypress.json
├── tests/
│   └── unit/
│       └── example.spec.js
├── jest.config.js
├── package.json
├── src/
│   └── components/
│       └── ExampleComponent.vue
├── node_modules/
└── ...
```

By following these steps, you've successfully set up a robust testing environment for your Vue.js-based PWA. Now, you can proceed to write comprehensive tests to ensure the reliability and functionality of your application.

11.2 Unit Testing Vue Components

Unit testing is an essential practice in software development, ensuring that individual components of your application behave as expected. In the context of Vue.js and Progressive Web Apps (PWAs), unit tests help verify the functionality and reliability of your Vue components. This subchapter explores how to set up and execute unit tests for Vue components using popular testing libraries and provides examples to guide you through the process.

Understanding Unit Testing in Vue.js

Unit tests focus on small, isolated pieces of code. For Vue.js applications, this generally means testing individual Vue components. The goal is to ensure that each component works correctly in isolation before integrating it into the larger application.

A typical unit test for a Vue component might involve: - Rendering the component. - Interacting with the component (e.g., clicking a button). - Asserting that the component behaves as expected.

Setting Up Your Testing Environment

Before you can start writing unit tests, you need to set up your testing environment. If you followed the steps outlined in subchapter 11.1, you should already have the necessary tools installed. Vue Test Utils and Jest are popular choices for testing Vue components.

To install these tools, you can use npm:

```
npm install @vue/test-utils jest vue-jest babel-jest --save-dev
```

Next, configure Jest by creating a file named `jest.config.js` in the root of your project:

```js
module.exports = {
  moduleFileExtensions: ['js', 'json', 'vue'],
  transform: {
    '.*\\.(vue)$': 'vue-jest',
    '^.+\\.js$': 'babel-jest',
  },
  testMatch: ['**/tests/unit/**/*.spec.js']
};
```

Writing Your First Unit Test

Let's start by writing a simple unit test for a `Counter` component. This component has a button that increments a count value when clicked.

First, create the `Counter.vue` component:

```vue
<template>
  <div>
    <p>{{ count }}</p>
    <button @click="increment">Increment</button>
  </div>
</template>

<script>
export default {
  data() {
    return {
      count: 0,
    };
  },
  methods: {
    increment() {
      this.count += 1;
    },
  },
};
</script>
```

Next, create a test file named `Counter.spec.js` in the `tests/unit` directory:

```js
import { shallowMount } from '@vue/test-utils';
import Counter from '@/components/Counter.vue';

describe('Counter.vue', () => {
  it('increments count when button is clicked', async () => {
    const wrapper = shallowMount(Counter);
    expect(wrapper.text()).toContain('0');

    await wrapper.find('button').trigger('click');
    expect(wrapper.text()).toContain('1');
  });
});
```

In this test: 1. We use `shallowMount` to render the Counter component in isolation. 2. We check the initial text to ensure the count starts at 0. 3. We simulate a button click and check that the count increments to 1.

Mocking Dependencies

Sometimes, your components depend on external services or complex logic that makes direct testing difficult. In these cases, mocking can be helpful. Vue Test Utils provides utilities for mocking props, methods, and other dependencies.

Consider a `MessageFetcher` component that fetches messages from an API:

```
<template>
  <div>
    <p>{{ message }}</p>
    <button @click="fetchMessage">Fetch Message</button>
  </div>
</template>

<script>
export default {
  data() {
    return {
      message: '',
    };
  },
  methods: {
    async fetchMessage() {
      const response = await fetch('http://api.example.com/message');
      const data = await response.json();
      this.message = data.text;
    },
  },
};
</script>
```

You can mock the `fetchMessage` method in your unit test:

```
import { shallowMount } from '@vue/test-utils';
import MessageFetcher from '@/components/MessageFetcher.vue';

describe('MessageFetcher.vue', () => {
  it('fetches and displays message on button click', async () => {
    const wrapper = shallowMount(MessageFetcher);
    const mockMessage = 'Hello, world!';

    jest.spyOn(wrapper.vm, 'fetchMessage').mockResolvedValue({
      text: mockMessage,
    });

    await wrapper.vm.fetchMessage();
    expect(wrapper.vm.message).toBe(mockMessage);
    expect(wrapper.text()).toContain(mockMessage);
  });
});
```

Testing Vuex-Connected Components

If your component interacts with a Vuex store, you'll need to mock the store in your tests. Suppose you have a `UserProfile` component that displays a user's name from the Vuex store:

```
<template>
  <div>
    <p>{{ userName }}</p>
  </div>
</template>

<script>
import { mapState } from 'vuex';
export default {
  computed: {
    ...mapState(['userName']),
  },
};
</script>
```

Here's how you mock the Vuex store in your unit test:

```
import { shallowMount, createLocalVue } from '@vue/test-uti
ls';
import Vuex from 'vuex';
import UserProfile from '@/components/UserProfile.vue';

const localVue = createLocalVue();
localVue.use(Vuex);

describe('UserProfile.vue', () => {
  let store;
  let state;

  beforeEach(() => {
    state = {
      userName: 'John Doe',
    };
    store = new Vuex.Store({
      state,
    });
  });

  it('displays the user name from the store', () => {
    const wrapper = shallowMount(UserProfile, { store, loca
lVue });
    expect(wrapper.text()).toContain('John Doe');
  });
});
```

Conclusion

Unit testing Vue components is a crucial step in ensuring the reliability and maintainability of your Progressive Web App. By using tools like Vue Test Utils and Jest, you can easily write and run unit tests to validate your components' behavior. Effective unit testing helps catch issues early, simplifies debugging, and improves code quality, ultimately leading to a better user experience for your PWA.

11.3 End-to-End Testing with Cypress

End-to-End (E2E) testing is crucial for ensuring the reliability and performance of your Progressive Web App (PWA). In this section, we will leverage Cypress, a powerful and user-friendly E2E testing framework, to validate user interactions and the functionality of our Vue.js PWA.

What is Cypress?

Cypress is an open-source testing tool that provides a comprehensive environment for writing, running, and debugging tests. It integrates seamlessly with modern web applications and offers features like time-travel debugging, automatic wait, and a powerful assertion library.

Setting Up Cypress

To get started with Cypress, you must first install it within your Vue.js project. Run the following command to install Cypress via npm:

```
npm install cypress --save-dev
```

Once installed, initialize Cypress in your project:

```
npx cypress open
```

This command will open the Cypress Test Runner and create a directory called `cypress/` in your project. This directory contains fixtures, integration tests, and configuration files.

Writing Your First Cypress Test

Let's create a Cypress test to verify that the homepage of your PWA loads correctly. First, navigate to the `cypress/integration` folder and create a new file called `home.spec.js`.

Within this file, write the following test:

```
describe('Homepage', () => {
  it('should load successfully', () => {
    cy.visit('http://localhost:8080');   // URL of your PWA
    cy.contains('Welcome to Your Vue.js App');
  });
});
```

This test performs the following steps:

97. `describe`: Groups tests related to the homepage.
98. `it`: Defines an individual test with a human-readable description.
99. `cy.visit`: Loads the specified URL (in this case, the homepage of your PWA).
100. `cy.contains`: Asserts that the text "Welcome to Your Vue.js App" is present on the page.

Running Cypress Tests

You can run Cypress tests either via the Cypress Test Runner GUI or through the command line for Continuous Integration (CI):

To use the GUI:

```
npx cypress open
```

To run tests via the command line:

```
npx cypress run
```

Interacting with Elements

Cypress provides powerful commands to interact with and test various elements on your page. For example, to test a login form, you can write the following:

```
describe('Login Page', () => {
  it('should allow a user to login', () => {
    cy.visit('http://localhost:8080/login');

    cy.get('input[name="username"]').type('user123');
    cy.get('input[name="password"]').type('password123');

    cy.get('button[type="submit"]').click();

    // Verify that the URL changes to the dashboard
    cy.url().should('include', '/dashboard');

    // Verify that the dashboard page contains the username
    cy.contains('Welcome, user123');
  });
});
```

In this example: 1. `cy.get`: Selects elements using CSS selectors. 2. `type`: Simulates user input. 3. `click`: Simulates a click event. 4. `cy.url`: Asserts that the URL includes '/dashboard'. 5. `cy.contains`: Verifies that the username is displayed on the dashboard page post-login.

Debugging Cypress Tests

Cypress offers excellent debugging features: - **Time Travel**: Click on commands in the Cypress Test Runner to see snapshots of the application at each step. - **Console Logs**: Cypress logs provide detailed information about each command's execution. - **Debugger Statements**: Place a `debugger` statement in your tests to pause execution and inspect the state manually.

```
cy.get('input[name="username"]').type('user123').debug();
```

Conclusion

End-to-End testing with Cypress in your Vue.js PWA ensures that not only individual components work correctly but also that the entire application functions as expected from the user's perspective. By incorporating Cypress into your testing strategy, you enhance the robustness and maintainability of your Progressive Web App, providing users with a seamless experience.

11.4 Debugging Common Issues

Debugging common issues in a Progressive Web App (PWA) built with Vue.js requires a multifaceted approach. In this section, we will cover several typical problems and their corresponding debugging strategies, ensuring you have the tools to efficiently track down and fix issues in your application. We'll discuss dealing with issues related to Vue.js components, service workers, caching, and offline behavior.

Debugging Vue.js Components

When debugging Vue.js components, it's essential to leverage Vue Devtools – an official browser extension for Chrome and Firefox that provides advanced tools for debugging Vue.js applications.

Installation and Usage

To install Vue Devtools, visit the Chrome Web Store or the Firefox Add-ons site and search for "Vue.js Devtools." Once installed, you can access it via the browser's developer tools panel.

Inspecting Components

Vue Devtools allows you to inspect the component hierarchy, view component data, and see reactive properties in real time.

```
// Example Component
<template>
  <div>
    <p>{{ message }}</p>
    <button @click="updateMessage">Update Message</button>
  </div>
</template>

<script>
export default {
  data() {
    return {
      message: "Hello, World!"
    };
  },
  methods: {
    updateMessage() {
      this.message = "Hello, Vue!";
    }
  }
};
</script>
```

With Vue Devtools, you can inspect the `message` property and see it update when the button is clicked, ensuring your methods and data bindings are functioning correctly.

Common Vue.js Issues

101. **Uncaught TypeError**: Often happens when trying to access properties that do not exist. Use Vue Devtools to ensure your data properties are defined and correctly spelled.

102. **Component Prop Validation**: Ensure that the properties passed to components match the expected types and ranges.

```
props: {
  count: {
    type: Number,
    default: 0,
    validator: value => value >= 0
  }
}
```

Debugging Service Workers

Service workers are critical to PWAs, providing offline capabilities and caching. However, they can introduce unique challenges.

Checking Service Worker Registration

Ensure your service worker is correctly registered:

```
if ('serviceWorker' in navigator) {
  navigator.serviceWorker.register('/service-worker.js')
    .then(registration => {
      console.log('ServiceWorker registration successful with scope: ', registration.scope);
    })
    .catch(error => {
      console.log('ServiceWorker registration failed: ', error);
    });
}
```

Check for errors in the console to ensure that the service worker is registered and active.

Common Service Worker Issues

103. **Service Worker Not Updating**: This might be due to caching. Use `skipWaiting` and `self.clients.claim()` to force the service worker to update immediately.

```
self.addEventListener('install', event => {
  event.waitUntil(
    caches.open(CACHE_NAME).then(cache => {
      return cache.addAll(URLS_TO_CACHE);
    }).then(() => {
      return self.skipWaiting();
    })
  );
});

self.addEventListener('activate', event => {
  event.waitUntil(
    self.clients.claim()
  );
});
```

2. **Fetching Failures**: Check network responses and ensure your fetch event handlers are correctly catching and handling network errors.

```
self.addEventListener('fetch', event => {
  event.respondWith(
    caches.match(event.request)
      .then(response => {
        return response || fetch(event.request)
      })
      .catch(error => {
        console.error('Fetch failed; returning offline page instead.', error);
        return caches.match('/offline.html');
      })
  );
});
```

Caching Problems

Proper caching strategies are vital for optimizing load times and offline functionality.

Inspecting Caches

You can inspect the caches using the Application panel in Chrome DevTools. Navigate to `Application > Cache Storage` to view and manage cached assets.

Common Caching Issues

104. **Stale Content**: Use cache busting techniques or the `Cache-Control` HTTP header to ensure updated assets are fetched.

```
fetch('/api/data', {
  headers: {
    'Cache-Control': 'no-cache'
  }
});
```

2. **Cache Overgrowth**: Periodically clean up old caches to save space and ensure that users have the latest versions of your assets.

```
self.addEventListener('activate', event => {
  const cacheWhitelist = [CACHE_NAME];
  event.waitUntil(
    caches.keys().then(cacheNames => {
      return Promise.all(
        cacheNames.map(cacheName => {
          if (!cacheWhitelist.includes(cacheName)) {
            return caches.delete(cacheName);
          }
        })
      );
    })
  );
});
```

Addressing Offline Capabilities

Offline capabilities are a fundamental aspect of PWAs. Test offline functionality by toggling the "Offline" checkbox in Chrome DevTools' Network panel.

Handling Offline Issues

105. **Network-Dependent Features**: Ensure that components gracefully handle offline scenarios, perhaps by showing user notifications.

```
if (!navigator.online) {
  alert('You are offline. Some features may not be availabl
e.');
}
```

2. **Fallback Pages**: Provide fallback pages for critical resources.

```
self.addEventListener('fetch', event => {
  if (event.request.mode === 'navigate' && event.request.ur
l.endsWith('.html')) {
    event.respondWith(
      fetch(event.request).catch(() => {
        return caches.match('/offline.html');
      })
    );
  }
});
```

By addressing these common issues with effective debugging strategies, you can ensure your Progressive Web App built with Vue.js remains robust, performant, and user-friendly across various conditions and environments.

12. Glossary

Glossary for "Building Progressive Web Apps with Vue.js"

Progressive Web Apps (PWAs)

A type of application software delivered through the web that is built using common web technologies including HTML, CSS, and JavaScript. PWAs are intended to work on any platform that uses a standards-compliant browser. They offer functionalities like offline access, push notifications, and performance enhancements traditionally associated with native applications.

Vue.js

An open-source JavaScript framework for building user interfaces and single-page applications. Vue.js is designed to be incrementally adoptable, meaning that if you have an existing project, you can start small and integrate Vue.js components without needing to rewrite the entire codebase.

Development Environment

Refers to the setup of tools and software necessary for building, testing, and debugging applications. For Vue.js, this typically involves Node.js, npm, Vue CLI, a code editor like VS Code, and browser development tools.

Vue.js App

A project or application built using the Vue.js framework. It consists of components, directives, and a reactive data binding system that displays data updates in real-time.

Progressive Web App Features

These include capabilities such as offline-first operation, add to home screen, push notifications, background synchronization, and fast loading times, which collectively contribute to the user experience by making web apps more reliable and engaging.

Vue.js Components

Reusable, self-contained units in Vue.js that encapsulate their HTML, CSS, and JavaScript. Components make it easier to manage and scale applications, as they promote modularity and separation of concerns.

Vuex

A state management pattern and library for Vue.js applications. Vuex provides a centralized store for all the components in an application, ensuring a predictable way to mutate the state and allowing for better state management in large-scale applications.

Service Workers

Scripts that run in the background and allow for features that do not need a web page or user interaction. They are essential for enabling PWA features like offline capabilities, background sync, and push notifications.

Offline Capabilities

The ability for a web application to function without an internet connection. This is typically achieved by caching essential resources and data using service workers and leveraging browser storage APIs.

Performance Optimization

Techniques and practices used to improve the speed and efficiency of a web application. This can include code splitting, lazy loading, image optimization, and leveraging browser caching, among other strategies.

Testing

The process of evaluating a PWA to ensure it meets the required standards and works as expected. This typically involves unit tests, integration tests, and end-to-end tests to identify and fix bugs before deployment.

Debugging

The process of identifying, analyzing, and resolving issues or bugs in an application. Debugging tools for Vue.js and PWAs often include browser DevTools, Vue Devtools, and various logging techniques.

Glossary

A list or collection of terms with definitions, usually found at the end of a book or document, meant to provide explanations and context for specific terminology used within the text.

www.ingramcontent.com/pod-product-compliance
Lightning Source LLC
Chambersburg PA
CBHW052311220526
45472CB00001B/65